My Times & Life

My Times & Life

A Historian's Progress through a Contentious Age

Morton Keller

HOOVER INSTITUTION PRESS
STANFORD UNIVERSITY | STANFORD, CALIFORNIA

www.hoover.org

Hoover Institution Press Publication No. 594

Hoover Institution at Leland Stanford Junior University, Stanford, California, 94305-6010

First printing 2010
16   15   14   13   12   11   10   9   8   7   6   5   4   3   2   1

Manufactured in the United States of America

The paper used in this publication meets the minimum Requirements of the American National Standard for Information Sciences—Permanence of Paper for Printed Library Materials, ANSI/NISO Z39.48-1992. ⊗

Library of Congress Cataloging-in-Publication Data
Keller, Morton.
My times and life : a historian's progress through a contentious age / Morton Keller.
    p. cm.—(Hoover Institution Press publication series ; no. 594)
ISBN 978-0-8179-1184-3 (cloth : alk. paper)
ISBN 978-0-8179-1186-7 (e-book)
    1. Keller, Morton.   2. Historians—United States—Biography.
3. United States—Historiography.   4. United States—History—
20th century.   I. Title.
E175.5.K45A3   2010
907.2′02—dc22   2010031848
[B]

For the family—all of it.

CONTENTS

Introduction

V LADIMIR NABOKOV peremptorily ordered his memoir to *Speak, Memory*. A friend planned to call his recollections *At Memory's Gate* (*At*, not *Through*). Memory is not simple; nor is it simply desirable.

Like others in my sunset time of life, I am drawn to a recollection of times past, an exercise that uncomfortably resembles a wake: *my* wake. The all-but-universal temptation to set down what led to one's current condition, and the fact that I'm the only one around who can speak with some authority on the subject, has led me to offer this ramble through my past.

As a historian I of course welcome, even woo, memory. It is not only my stock in trade but, I firmly believe, a defining feature of human sentience. And yet . . . Do I really want to swing wide the doors of memory? Cautious judges like to warn that upholding a particular legal principle or practice would "open the floodgates of litigation." My similar reservation about memory is that, unleashed, it's like a rogue elephant. There's no telling where it will go, no way of assuring that it will favor the wheat over the chaff of one's life.

Who knows what acts better done than undone, or better undone than done—what bons mots that went bad—will surface? Memory is the worst of all primal (or, as a historian would say, primary) sources. It plays havoc with failing synapses, and with feral cunning feeds on the powerful human desire to preserve—indeed, to gussy up—one's self. Will memory in this case fit the English schoolgirl's definition of lying: an abomination unto the Lord, but an ever-ready friend in time of trouble?

Let's see how it goes.

A memoir always requires (for the reader, if not for the author) some convincing justification for chopping down all those trees. That is especially so in a case like mine, where there is no obvious rationale—no spectacularly successful, or failed, or lurid life. I have no great triumphs to gloat over or disasters to rationalize, no secrets to reveal or scandal to tell. Mine is a tale that belongs to that always attractive, but hardly momentous, American saga of respectable achievement from relatively humble origins.

But I have lived my life in interesting times. The Great Depression, World War II, the cold war, the sixties, and 9/11 add up to something more than a run-of-the-mill run of history. So my title puts first things first: *My Times and Life*. As far as I can tell, this is a title not previously used, as contrasted with the all-too-common *My Life and Times*: a nice measure of the egotism that drives most memoirists.

One other talking point: I have been through eight-plus decades as a solid, unequivocal, dues-paying member of perhaps the least observed of all social groups—the middle class. Workers and proles get a generally respectable press from the writers and academics who have looked at them over the past hundred and fifty years or so. The upper class and the literary and intellectual elites often have a rougher time of it. But they can count on recurrently admiring treatment as well. Wealth, fame, genius, and outrageous attitudes and behavior have their attractions. And even when the golden people are being savaged, there is often a mixture of envy and schadenfreude that reminds us why, for all their manifest absurdity, royals and aristocrats command such widespread interest.

Middling people are not likely to elicit strong responses. We tend to be seen (if seen at all) as part of the neutral social backdrop against which the dramas of the poor and the rich, or the greatly good and the greatly bad, are avidly observed.

So this is an account of a not extraordinary life played out in extraordinary times. Even so, it is a story with a wider resonance. That brings us to the primary reason for my taking on the task of telling my tale. Most of it echoes the experience, the beliefs, and the values of a large chunk—perhaps a plurality—of my generation.

North Carolinians like to describe their state as a valley of humility between those two mountains of conceit, Virginia and South Carolina. With much (though not all) of its normative quality removed, something similar might be said of me and my contemporaries: born too late to be part of the Greatest Generation that fought and won World War II; born too early to be part of the baby boom generation that (in its own view) transformed late twentieth-century America.

To be a reasonably successful member of a not notably distinguished generation is hardly to be among the best-situated claimants for public attention or admiration. But as Sherlock

Holmes liked to say, there may be a point or two of interest in the tale I have to tell.

Before doing so, I owe heartfelt thanks to those who did their best to make this account less of a sow's ear and more of a silk purse: my wife, Phyllis, and dear friends and fellow-historians Steve Thernstrom and Aida Donald. They struggled manfully (and womanfully) to sharpen my understanding of my times and life. The dull edges remaining are my own alone.

CHAPTER ONE

Beginnings

MIDDLE-CLASS FAMILIES tend not to leave a fulsome written record behind them. I can tap no store of letters or memoirs from friends or relatives, near or distant. Indeed, aside from myself there are no immediate family memory-carriers to draw upon. My mother had no siblings; my father had a brother, considerably older, usually distant in space, long gone, leaving no extended family around when I arrived on the scene. Except for my mother's socially remote immigrant parents, there was no human context in which to embed family memory, only a scattering of my parents' friends. The short and simple annals of the poor can be shared in good measure by the middle class.

The *primary* primary source of my ancestry and youth turns out to be photos. These are the most common record-keeping device of twentieth-century American families, and certainly the least subject to the constraints of talent or skill. In our own time, the swift ascent of digital computer photography has taken the Kodak era's every-man-his-own-picture-taker appeal to a new level of participatory creativity. This peculiarly democratic, contemporary impulse to (usually talent-free) expression may be seen as well in those popular pastimes macramé and jogging, and most fruitfully in the domains of e-mailing and texting, where neither high literacy nor solid substance is part of the price of admission.

My father came to America from an exotic locale: turn-of-the-century Palestine. He was born into a family that had been there since the early nineteenth century. In the wake of Napoleon a small aliyah of several thousand devout East European Jews made their way to the Holy Land: a post-Enlightenment reaction by the Unenlightened. There is a family legend—maybe a *true* legend—that the pioneering ancestor crossed the Black Sea in a small sailboat on the way to Palestine.

The family initially was centered in Safed, an old center of Jewish learning and mysticism. It was rich as well in plagues and earthquakes, which perhaps explains why my father's father wound up in Jerusalem and other members of the family took to cultivating orange groves. I remember an occasional letter in the 1930s from my father's family (no one closer than cousins of some remove) who went around armed against Arabs, already at war with these "intruders" (whose Palestinian roots in fact probably antedated most of their attackers).

I made my first trip to Israel in the 1970s and met my family, whose patriarch was Aaron Keller, a second cousin and retired farmer who had tracked me down in the course of a trip around the world, and thus reconnected me to this lost ancestry. We had a family gathering; to my wife Phyllis's astonishment, another distant cousin of mine, close to my own age, displayed bodily movements and facial mannerisms eerily like my own.

It was a social as well as an economic statement that the family dwelt in a compound of several houses on Gluskin Street in the middle of Rehovot, one of Israel's older Zionist-founded communities. It was initially an agricultural market town (hence, probably, my family's presence there), and later the home of the Weizmann Institute, Israel's leading science research center (with which my relatives apparently had nothing to do). Their houses were substantial by Israeli standards. And the British police headquarters nearby, built during the British Mandate, stood on land bought from the family.

These Israeli relatives were an eye-opener in other ways, too. They were unlike any other Israelis I met in the course of my life: neither kibbutzim socialists nor Tel Aviv entrepreneurs nor Hebrew University academics, but the Israeli equivalent of South African Boers or Algerian *colons*: longtime residents, steeped in an agricultural past, contemptuous of both the Arabs and the latter-day secular/socialist Zionists who surrounded them. They referred to the Tel Aviv headquarters of the Histadrut, the major Israeli labor federation, as "the Kremlin." When I met them in the 1970s, they spoke little or no English, a notable achievement in modern Israel.

Meeting these *landsmen* sharpened my understanding of my father. He was not the easiest of men; he had an artist's prickly temperament. Born in 1889, he spent his youth in Jerusalem, where his father, an artisan of some ability, had a crafts and souvenir store. Early on he was enrolled in a *cheder*: a religious school whose obscurantism in that time and place can only be imagined. In any event, in the early 1900s his artist's impulse drove him out of the *cheder*, indeed out of Jerusalem and Palestine, to—where else?—Paris.

He studied art there (no further information was vouchsafed me when I was growing up) and came to America a few years later. An additional lure: his older brother was a sculptor who emigrated to America without his family and returned to Palestine some years later. The shipping manifest of the *SS Louisiane*, out of Le Havre, tells me that my father arrived in New York on June 11, 1909. His brother, Abraham, met him and contrived to whisk the new arrival onto land without his being subjected to the rigors of Ellis Island.

I pore over the sepia-tinted handful of photographs from my father's Palestine that have come down to me, seeking to tease out clues to my roots. In a 1901 picture my early-teen father, looking much as I did at the same age, stands on the right, beside his considerably older brother. Posed before them are my father's mother, with his brother's wife on the left, displaying their youngest child; the other two are draped around their grandmother. (I know no names; I deduce the relationships.) [Plate 1]

My father's father was dead by the time of this photo. But there is an earlier image of him proudly posed behind his model of the Rothschild Hospital in Jerusalem, which was opened in 1888 as the first Jewish-identified hospital outside of the Old City. [Plate 2] The building is still there, now housing the Hadassah College of Technology: a physical representation of the evolution of the Jewish presence in Jerusalem from the introspective Jerusalem of my father's youth to a larger, proto-national identity.

That model of my grandfather's is real to me: I saw it in the 1970s when I visited my father's relatives in Rehovot. The roof came off to reveal minute doctors, nurses, and patients engaged in the *ronde* of hospital life. It was done with some skill, and speaks of the combination of craftsmanship and souvenir-selling that was my paternal grandfather's livelihood and of the artistic talent that, in different form, was transmitted to his son. (But then the genetic strain stopped cold. Neither I, my children, or grandchildren—save perhaps one—have artistic talent.)

This is about all I know of my father's life in Palestine before that day in 1909 when he departed, to return only twice for brief visits after World Wars I and II. My mother's family—about whom I know even less—had a more familiar immigrant experience. My maternal grandparents made their way to the United States in the late 1800s, part of that vast, faceless mass driven out of the Russian and Austro-Hungarian empires by worsening anti-Semitism and economic conditions, drawn by the lure of *Der Goldener Land.*

My recollection of my mother's parents (she had no siblings, aunts or uncles, or cousins) stretches from the 1930s to their deaths in the 1950s. Their major distinction was in the difference between their personalities. My maternal grandfather, Aaron Sherman, was a gentle, other-worldly man. He was a skilled tailor and made a reasonably good living working for Hattie Carnegie, an upscale women's clothing entrepreneur not unlike the cosmetics diva Helena Rubenstein. She appealed, if not to the carriage trade, at least to the taxi trade: the growing number of (primarily Jewish) women sufficiently well-off to buy expensive clothes and have them skillfully fitted by craftsmen like my grandfather.

My mother's mother, Clara Sherman, was another story: what today would be called a piece of work. She came to America from a Romanian *shtetl*: from where, when, and at what age I don't know. In my recollection she remains a classic non-assimilated immigrant, with little English (Yiddish was her mode of discourse) and even less connection to the American world around her.

I don't know what tribulations along the old immigrant trail soured her. I do recall her manic insistence on having huge dinners to which various "uncles" and "cousins"—few if any with true family connections—flocked; a free meal was not lightly skipped in those days. What I remember most of all was the gulf in temperament that made her a constant trial to my mother who, guilt-driven, would spend long hours on the subway paying dutiful but inevitably painful, tension-fraught visits.

In my time, my maternal grandparents lived in an attached row house in Brooklyn's East New York neighborhood, an area since obliterated by the ravages of the social decline that hit that part of the city during the late twentieth century. Before that they resided, I surmise, in New York's upper West Side, close to Hattie Carnegie's original store.

Sometime after World War II, in a monumental act of folly, my grandfather opened his own tailoring shop across the street from Loehmann's dress store at Sterling Place and Bedford Avenue in Brooklyn, and moved to East New York. This pioneering shop, in which women could get high-fashion dresses at knock-down prices, led to forms of group conduct immortalized in Erma Bombeck's great ethnographic study, *All I Know About Animal Behavior I Learned in Loehmann's Dressing Room.* The store didn't bother with niceties such as alterations. My grandfather hoped to tap that trade with his new shop. But saintliness is not the high road to commercial success. Until his death in the 1950s he struggled to make a living, which did little to temper my grandmother's sourness.

Where to begin my own saga? Like the nation to whose history I've devoted my career, it properly begins at the beginning, with a Declaration denoting my Independence: not from unwanted

Imperial rule but from my mother's womb. Mine was not an eloquent document, but it was signed, and legal, and official: a birth certificate. It announced that Mortimer Keller was born on March 1, 1929, at St. John's Hospital in Brooklyn, New York. It bore the signatures not of the likes of Thomas Jefferson, John Adams, and Benjamin Franklin, but the less historically resonant James J. Walker, mayor of the City of New York, Commissioner of Health Louis I. Harris, and Registrar William H. Guilfoyle, M.D.

Like any historical document, it calls for context and interpretation. Someone born in 1929 inherits a burden of historical resonance comparable to those who saw the light of day in 1914. Each of those years marked The End of an Era and the commencement of a new one: the onset of the Great Depression, the beginning of the Great War. However unwanted, those disasters were part of the birthright of everyone born under their stars.

Why did I enter life in St. John's, an Episcopalian hospital, when Brooklyn had its fair share of Jewish ones? Perhaps convenience: the hospital was at 1545 Atlantic Avenue, fairly close to my parents' address, relatively upscale 320 Eastern Parkway. But Brooklyn Jewish Hospital was not much further away at 555 Prospect Place in Prospect Heights. My mother's budding assimilationist impulse may well have been at play.

For reasons lost to my family's (non-)history, my parents named me Mortimer. The appellation was quite popular, among the top one hundred given names in the early twentieth century. But it was already in steep decline by 1929.

It was a name of Old French origin—on the face of it, not likely to attract a Jewish family derived from Palestine and Romania (though my father did put in some time in Paris). God only knows what mix of upwardly mobile inclinations and romanticism went into what I assume was my mother's choice.

True, the name does literally mean "dead sea," suggesting a faint link with the Old Testament and my father's Holy Land origins. But its actual derivation appears to have been from a stagnant lake on a baronial French family's lands. One of my few first-name counterparts, publisher Mortimer Zuckerman, was born in Montreal in 1937, the provinciality of the birthplace perhaps accounting for the persistence of a near-archaic name.

Early on in my life, Mortimer morphed into Morton, an easy Anglicization. Here we plunge still deeper into the assimilationist woods. Morton was a slightly less popular name than Mortimer in the early twentieth century, slightly more so later. It was a name solidly English in its origin, though it did have an exotic original meaning: Moor Town. Presumably it was less redolent than Mortimer of—what? Out-of-dateness? Foreignness? Jewishness? The most notable Morton of my time was the decisively non-Jewish popular singer Morton Downey (born 1901), whose son Morton Downey Jr. (born 1932) would later be a celebrity television talk show host. Or was the name change my doing, a response to playground taunts over the by-now obsolete Mortimer? Search me. (If you do, you won't find an answer.)

Then, in rapid turn, came another change: from Morton to Mickey, so widely used by family and friends that it became as much a name as a nickname. This sets off yet more obvious assimilationist signals. Two historian friends a few years older than me had similar socially neutral monikers. Harvard colonial historian Bernard Bailyn was, and is, for all purposes and to almost all comers, "Bud." So was my Brandeis colleague Marvin Meyers. Ours was a generation of Jews whose more tradition-bound parents adhered to established naming rules—Mortimer, Bernard, Marvin—but whose aspiring offspring sought a more readily acceptable identity in their common form of address.

This was even more widely true of last names. Mine—Keller—was adopted by my father's Palestinian family, in place of an earlier name lost to memory, when they became subjects of the Austro-Hungarian monarchy as a protective device against on-the-ground Ottoman rule. (I'm sure the Emperor Franz Josef was pleased.) And no doubt the Bailyns and the Meyerses, a generation or two back, called themselves something more Jewish Old World than that.

Eight months after my birth, the stock market crashed. I am quite confident that there was no causal connection. But it is solid historical fact that October 29, 1929—that day when the stock market definitively informed America's Dorothys that they no longer lived in the jolly old land of Oz, but were on their way back to woeful Kansas—was also the day of my parents' fifth wedding anniversary. My father, as one of the few surviving bits of family lore has it, kept from my mother on that happy day the fact that he had been hit hard indeed by unfortunate events downtown.

Of course neither my parents (nor, need I say, I) had any notion of how much, and what kind, of history lay in wait. Indeed, I entered into my time in a context, both family and social, of overwhelming, unalloyed ordinariness: that vast, vague, unsung entity called the middle-middle class, devoid of the violence or affective pathos of workers, or the eccentricities or emoluments of upper-middle folk (to say nothing of those even higher up the social food chain).

Most constructions of society dwell not on the stratum into which I was born, but on the layers above and below: on the miseries (and virtues) of the poor and almost-poor, and the comforts and (usually self-imposed) torments of the rich and almost-rich. Ric Burns's *New York*, a Public Broadcasting Service documentary history of the city, unrelentingly dwelt on the sufferings of the poor and the excesses of the rich, at the cost of the more ambiguous life experience of what by the twentieth century would be the dominant class of New Yorkers.

But so it has been in the history-writing of my time. Why is it that as the modern United States turned definitively from a working-class to a middle-class society, its historians chose to dwell on the tails and not the peak of the social bell curve? That is a problem best left to students of the prevailing ideology of the academic class.

We were middle class in the American sense of being comfortable but hardly affluent, not in the English sense of being in fact quite well-off both financially and in the social pecking order. In this large and indeterminate category—like "post," as in "postmodern," a cop-out term of social categorization resistant to more precise definition—we occupied a solid economic niche. I estimate that as a self-employed commercial artist my father earned around $3,000 to $5,000 annually during the Depression years, which must have put us well within the top ten percent of American family incomes.

My father appears to have readily found his way as a commercial artist in New York. He began by drawing advertisements for the Yiddish press. I have one of them: a sketch of a devout, heavily bearded Jew sipping a cup of coffee, presumably announcing (in Yiddish?) that it was good to the last drop—as well it should have been, since this was an ad for Maxwell House Coffee. [Plate 3]

He also earned income by drawing postcards to be used by new immigrants to assure their left-behind families that all was well in the New World. [Plate 4] Possessors of commercially viable talents—artists like my father, writers, Tin Pan Alley composers—had a measurably easier time of it than most other immigrants.

He became a citizen in November 1914, five years after his arrival: he sought that status as quickly as he could. Flat feet kept him out of the Army in World War I, and by the 1920s he was quite the man about Mayor Jimmy Walker's New York town. His studio was on Park Row, then the Fleet Street of the New York press. [Plate 5] He even had a car during those piping years before I, and then the Depression, came along, though never again.

How he met my mother, and why they married, I don't know. He was a dozen years older than her, but his attractions—a good income and a flourishing career as a commercial artist—are obvious enough. And my mother was a handsome woman, American-born, an unusually talented pianist who had actually gone to college (I think Adelphi) for a year or so. Thus they were, in the near-immigrant world to which they belonged, a mutually good match. They married in 1924 and honeymooned in fine 1920s style in Bermuda: not bad for an immigrant little more than a decade after his arrival. [Plate 6]

Their life in the 1920s reflected both my father's well-above-average income and my mother's well-above-average disposition to culture. They were consistent theatergoers, attending the popular musicals and serious dramas (Eugene O'Neill, etc.) of the time. They lived somewhere in Manhattan during those halcyon days before I came along.

Even after I arrived, and they resigned themselves to residing in more child-friendly Brooklyn, my parents maintained an unusually active cultural life. They belonged to the Brooklyn Academy of Music during the 1930s and I was aware of their attendance at Lowell Thomas's lectures on faraway places with strange-sounding names, and of frequent forays to the Broadway theater.

Despite intermittent piano lessons from an early age, my mother's heroic efforts to tap my musicality bore little fruit. You don't get blood from a stone. This was borne in on me in grade school, where—at least in New York City in the 1930s—the accepted mode in music classes was to sort pupils into three groups: tenors, sopranos, and listeners. The Deweyite progressive education approach that pervaded New York City's public schools in the 1930s presumably assumed that these were equally desirable states of being. I'll never really know: I landed unerringly in the third category.

Despite my lack of a musical ear, I was taken by my mother from an early age to the Young People's Concerts in Carnegie Hall, conducted from 1924 to the late 1930s by one Ernest Schelling, long before Leonard Bernstein came along and put a higher gloss on the enterprise. Piano lessons followed as night does day. My attendance at the Young People's Concerts and my forays at the piano no doubt fostered a lifelong pleasure in classical music. But my playing was as clueless as my listening. I did finally achieve a performance of sorts of Mozart's piano sonata in C major (K. 545), unerringly described by The Master himself as "for beginners." I still have an occasional twinge of remorse when I think of the captive audiences of parents forced to hear it at my teacher's annual presentation of her students' attainments.

Mine was perhaps the last generation when significant numbers of middle-class American youth were more or less forcibly exposed to classical music, with noticeable results. We were the core of the audience for such music during the post-World War II decades, until the inexorable cultural transformation of the 1960s and after threatened to consign that brand of musical taste to history's dustbin.

My father's Great Depression was not a time of stringency. As a freelance commercial artist he tapped a continuing, if shrunken, market for box designs or advertisements—whatever means were at hand to sell what goods there were to what customers there were.

His income in the Depression years was sufficient to support my mother's most notable excesses: a solid taste for fancy rags and a collector's urge for shoes, together with a distaste for house cleaning and a hunger for upward residential mobility that led us, every three or so years during my youngest days, to move out along Brooklyn's Ocean Avenue to the most recently constructed apartment house (which usually included rental-free months on a three-year lease). [Plates 7, 8, 9]

Early on, my father indulged in a form of social muscle-flexing not uncommon to Jewish middle-class families of the time: depositing the wife and kid(s) in the Mountains (the Catskills) or the Seashore (Rockaway and environs), self-sacrificially slaving and sweating in the sweltering city during the week and fleeing to the vacation haven on weekends.

In our case, the choice was the Mountains, not the Seashore. Perhaps that explains my lifelong preference for the sea, expressed in my joining the Navy at the tag end of the Korean War, a long-term interest in sailing, and in my maturity a summer place on a Cape Cod beach. And perhaps it explains an equally lifelong distaste (or lack of taste) for the charms of woods, mountains, and Inland in general.

I don't know for sure if my parents enacted this summertime ritual in the dark, distant years before I came along. I do know that I was part of it at an early age. Though detailed recollection has mercifully deserted me on this score, my mother, her mother, and I were summering on a Catskills farm in the early 1930s. I have a half-memory of being repelled by the hairs and other foreign matter in the unpasteurized milk direct from the cow that my mother (and, I suspect, coaching her, my grand-mother) forced on me: this was, after all, a family close to its immigrant roots.

I remember, too, having my mouth washed out with soap for uttering what must have been a pretty mild expletive. (At the tender age of four there was as yet little prospect of being really raunchy.) There is something touchingly timeless about that act: a symbolic cleansing that reeks of immemorial folk wisdom.

One other memory of those halcyon days: sitting interminably (for two hours, perhaps?) in an immobile bus headed back to the City on a broiling September 1934 day, while a National Recovery Administration parade went by. This is my first remembered contact with the larger social realities of my time.

As I look back, my childhood was an unusually isolated one. My parents, as I said, went out a lot, and had a (not large) circle of friends. I could hardly share in their play-and-lecture-going. And there was no extended family—no cousins, nephews, nieces—to compensate for my parents' intense focus on each other, a relationship in which I often had a marginal place.

My father was forty years old when I was born, and his tem-perament gave him little patience for the impositions of a young child. So my early youth was not an idyllic nor even a generally happy time. I recall frequent fights with my father, which my mother ineffectually tried to mediate. More than once I went through the childhood rebellion of threatening to run away from home, and a few times made it to the lobby of our apartment house, then to be stymied as to where to go next.

Nor did religion provide an enlarging context. My father, no doubt reacting to his Orthodox upbringing in Jerusalem, was fiercely anti-religious, to my mother's silent distress. We neither belonged to nor went to a synagogue. We did not observe the Sabbath; we neither had nor attended a Passover seder. My December toy bonanza appeared on Christmas morning, not as part of Hanukkah.

As my thirteenth birthday on March 1, 1942—time for the customary bar mitzvah—began to loom over the horizon, my mother put what pressure she could on my father to do something about my preparation. I recall an attempt on his part to teach me Hebrew, an effort that soon collapsed under the twin weights of my disinterest and his substantial lack of the patience and understanding called for. Instead, he relied on what I presume he remembered of his *cheder* pedagogy: threats and the assertion of authority (though not physical chastisement).

My thirteenth birthday came ever nearer, and my preparation remained nil. Some months before, in November 1941, my mother came down with pneumonia, which was not to be taken lightly in those pre-antibiotic days. For weeks she was encased in an oxygen tent at home, and no doubt pleaded with my father to get me some emergency bar mitzvah prepping. I vividly recall his confronting the rabbi of the temple in Forest Hills, where we now lived, and brusquely asking him if he could do a hurry-up job sufficient to get me through the ceremony. The rabbi not unreasonably resisted this idea, and the two had a loud and highly public argument. That put paid to my initiation into Jewish manhood.

What do I make of this experience today? It certainly did not impede the assimilationist impulse that was already building up in me. And my preteen and teenage years were spent with friends and activities in which the Jewish religion (as distinct from Jewishness as a cultural condition) was all but nonexistent.

I did go to Jewish camps from about the age of nine or ten; my parents clearly welcomed two months' respite from the rigors of child-rearing. But while I sat and mumbled through the camps' Saturday religious services, I felt no tie to, nor indeed had a yearning for, the communality of observance. This was not an uncommon condition among Jews of my generation. But my father's hostility to religion (shared with other immigrants of his time) and the relative social isolation of the life that he and my mother lived made my case an extreme one. It encouraged in me an assimilationist drive which led not to a rejection but to a constant downplaying of my Jewishness. More positively, it may have contributed to my eventual commitment to a career of studying, teaching, and writing mainstream American history, focusing on institutions and themes in which the Jewish element was not, to put it mildly, conspicuous.

As there was relatively little to attract me to home and family, I compensated in two, almost bipolar, ways: immersion in the street life of boys of my age, usually linked to intense friendships; and a hyperactive inner life, expressed in such forms as extended solitary play with construction kits. (I recall building quite elaborate ships and skyscrapers out of Stanlo, a simplified form of Erector set, and endless, complex battles and maneuvers with toy soldiers.) And increasingly I immersed myself in books from the local public library. Doctor Dolittle, Captain Blood, and Horatio Hornblower were more real to me than friends of my parents euphemistically labeled Aunt Gazie or Aunt Mattie. Perhaps this was the gate-opener to my ultimate plunge into the academic historian swamp.

In the late 1930s we moved to 1701 Albemarle Road in Flatbush, overlooking the BMT's Brighton Line subway (though mercifully that line traveled through a culvert). More to the point, we lived cheek by jowl with upper-middle-class country. Our spanking new apartment house looked out on a still grander life style. Behind us was the Knickerbocker Field Club, whose tennis courts represented a social level that could only be imagined. (I remember seeing Don Budge play an exhibition match there in 1938. I watched from our apartment window; the Club, I am confident, was closed to Jews.)

Literally across the (subway) tracks was a neighborhood of substantial houses and even an Estate: a baronial manse with (from a child's-eye view) rolling acres (though it turns out that it had only one). I always assumed that its owner belonged to the unattainable WASP elite. But no: it was the abode—of all people—of Israel Matz, a Lithuanian Jewish immigrant who founded the Ex-Lax Company in 1908 and grew rich on his bowel-clearing product.

Attending Public School 139 on Cortelyou Road, on the fringe of Upscaletown, I came to know several young scions of the area and entered into an intense play group relationship with them. We indulged in frenetic bike riding and roller skate hockey (appropriately spaced manhole covers made excellent goals) on their sequestered streets. I suppose this in theory might have been good early preparation for the Tour de France or emigration to Canada, neither of which, as things turned out, figured in my life.

I spent a lot of time with a pair of brothers, Hugh and John Hermann. What their father did I either didn't know or don't remember. What their uncle did is still vivid in my mind: nothing less than co-own the Marx toy company. When Christmas rolled around, they got the cream of that year's toy crop: remote-controlled planes and cars and other unimaginable delights.

The brothers treated each other with the delicacy and affection common to the breed: fights of unalloyed violence and hatred, snapping ketchup bottles in each other's direction so that at least some of the ensuing red stream would cross the opponent's face as it made its way around the table (and the dining room walls). What their mother—dimly recalled as a thoroughly assimilated woman of means—made of me I have no idea. I wasn't quite a project boy. After all, we lived in a relatively upscale apartment house (although I doubt the two mothers ever met). And I can't say that differences of income, culture, and class ever obsessed me. In any event, this boyhood idyll lasted only for a few years. First the older and then the younger Hermann went off to private school, and then to Harvard.

Otherwise my primary school days are pretty much a blur, lightened by a few remembered incidents.

One occurred in the fall of the election year of 1936. My school was home to hundreds of Jewish, Irish, and Italian kids, whose families were overwhelmingly for Franklin Delano Roosevelt, and a scattering of Protestants, who inclined to GOP candidate Alfred M. Landon. On a bright October morning the student body was lined up in the school yard, given small American flags, and loaded onto buses destined for Ocean Parkway, with instructions to wave their flags and cheer for the gentleman who would pass by in the open touring car.

Lieutenants of the Brooklyn Democratic organization most likely supervised the mobilization. (This was the same organization whose spokesman told a lesser-level officeholder worried that his name was not featured in the party's ads: "Have you noticed that when the ferry comes in from Staten Island it brings in a lot of garbage in its wake? Well, Roosevelt's your ferryboat.")

Another aspect of the P.S. 139 scene was a heavy stress on personal cleanliness. Children in general, the children of immigrants in particular, and Jewish immigrant children most particularly, were not generally regarded as paragons of cleanliness by our predominantly Irish Catholic schoolmarms. So school mornings began with an inspection of hands and fingernails, and those who failed to pass muster were sent home for repair work.

My on-the-swarthy-side skin color, and a longish walk to and from school festooned with tempting dirt clods begging to be thrown, were not conducive to passing this test. So more often than not my distraught mother had to scrub my hands down (with, as I remember, brushes of ever-increasing textural ferocity) and send me back to school with threats, admonitions, and pleas to keep them in their relatively pristine shape. But however much she scrubbed and buffed and protected my hands with gloves, I managed to dirty up my digits by the time I made it to the school grounds. There may well have been parent-teacher conferences on this matter.

Grafted to the traditional Irish Puritanism of the teaching staff was a thoroughly modern Progressivism in the school curriculum, presumably crafted by often Jewish, always earnest products of Columbia's Teachers College. The 1930s were the high noon of educational Progressivism, and P.S. 139 was not immune. The result was a bizarre mix of policy dictated by primarily Jewish disciples of John Dewey, implemented by predominantly Irish female teachers who, if anything, were disciples of the anti-Semitic demagogue Father Coughlin.

A high point of this educational mishmash was an eminently Progressive attempt to expose third graders to the benefits and delights of French. I well remember being confronted suddenly with the adventures of *Paul et Lizette dans le jardin*. (Just what they did there I don't recall.) This premature exercise in multiculturalism soon dribbled away, to join that vast host of lost causes that constitutes the greater part of the history of American public education.

Plate 1—Coming of Age in Palestine: My father (top right), his older, soon-to-go-to-America brother, wife and three children, and my father's mother (center).

Plate 2—My father's craftsman father and his *chef d' oeuvre*: a working model of the Rothschild Hospital in Jerusalem.

Plate 3—"Good to the Last Drop" in Yiddish: an ad by my father, newly arrived in America, for the immigrant press.

Plate 4—Making a buck in America: one of a series of illustrated postcards by my father, sold to immigrants wishing to stay in touch with the Old Country.

Plate 5—My commercial artist father in his 15 Park Row atelier.

Plate 6—The immigrant arrived: my parents on their 1924 Bermuda honeymoon.

Discovery Monument
Bermuda
Nov. 1924

Plate 7—The newest—and last—family acquisition, in the firm grip of his father.

Plate 8—The same, in the less controlling grip of his mother.

Plate 9—Still the same, more appropriately alone, in front of one of our Ocean Avenue apartment house stopovers.

Plate 10—In the late adolescence, posing before our Forest Hills row house.

Plate 12—A transient member of the officer class.

Plate 11—At Harvard graduate school, exuding false confidence.

Plate 13—The thoughtful scholar, appropriate to his Oxford setting.

Plate 14—Phyllis as Associate Dean of Faculty, exuding competence.

Plate 15—Phyllis receiving the Harvard Medal from former president Derek Bok, to polite acclaim.

Plate 16—In full maturity, addressing I don't remember who on I don't remember what.

Plate 17—Our fortieth anniversary, enjoying the occasion and our longevity.

Plate 18—Our fiftieth, with the family—all of it.

CHAPTER TWO

War and Peace

I N OCTOBER 1941, demonstrating an innate sense of history comparable to my having been born on the cusp of the Great Depression, my family and I hied ourselves to the suburban middle-class hinterland. Reporter-political analyst Samuel Lubell apostrophized that migration in *The Future of American Politics* (1952). He described what he called the Old Tenement Trails, stretching from the Lower East Side to Harlem or Yorkville in Manhattan; then to the East Bronx, "where trees stepped out of poems onto the streets"; then to the West Bronx . . . "[where] rolled true middle-class country. . . . janitors were called superintendents; apartment houses had lift elevators and parquet floors."

My family's migration began in Brooklyn, but otherwise was similar. Whether it took off from Brooklyn or the Bronx, Lubell noted, "the Tenement Trail has swung abruptly eastward to . . . Queens, which is currently the outermost fringe of New York's housing frontier. . . . From Rivington Street to Forest Hills in Queens is only a few miles. Historically the spanning of that distance was a social revolution."

We did in fact move to Forest Hills: but not, I hasten to add, into the Forest Hills usually identified with genteel, WASPy Long Island. Our destination was a newly built row house on the fringe of that geographical entity. Its address may have been Forest Hills, but its social reality was a newly forming suburbia, conceived and executed in accordance with the dictates of city zoners and the work of real estate developers. The two Forest Hillses consisted of an early twentieth-century native Protestant construct, and the subway-and-FHA-borne migration: heavily Jewish and Catholic, the children of the New Immigrants.

Our Forest Hills most definitely was not the Ozlike template of Old American gentility (or, if you prefer, gentileity) that I suspect resided in the mind's eye of my mother. But it securely fit into another construct: suburbia as the lodestone of the new middle class, a suburbia that was beginning to interject itself into the American consciousness as the Depression started to lift in the pre-Pearl Harbor years, and would explode into the most conspicuous American social reality in the post-War decades. In this sense our move to Forest Hills, on the eve of America's entry into World War II, was no less historically fraught than my birth on the eve of the Great Depression.

Before there was a Forest Hills, there was swamp and farmland, as in much of Queens, the New York City borough (as of 1898) east of Brooklyn on Long Island. The area that embraced Forest Hills bore the distinctly Realtor-unfriendly name of Whitepot. In 1906 the Cord Meyer Development Company bought six hundred acres of Whitepot land. Cord Meyer, a real estate developer who, like the pioneering frontiersmen of the nineteenth century, set out to bring civilization to the wilderness, played a large role in turning Queens from farmland into suburbia from the 1890s on.

In the immemorial practice of real estate upgrading, the tract was given the more toothsome name of Forest Hills. In part this was because of its closeness to Forest Park, a Frederick Law Olmsted-designed *plaisance* soon surrounded by suburbia. And in part, presumably, the name was chosen because forests and hills were inherently attractive natural goodies, certain to appeal to the upwardly mobile white collar-professional clientele that was the prime target of Realtor opportunity.

In 1909 the Cord Meyer Company sold 142 acres of its Forest Hills holdings to Margaret Sage, the widow of stockbroker-financier Russell Sage. Her Russell Sage Foundation was a classic construct of the Progressive Era, constantly embroiled in good works, among them hospitals, museums, and Russell Sage College. She intended to create a garden city of the sort celebrated by the English urban planner Ebenezer Howard, whose *Garden Cities of To-morrow* (1898) excited many of the reform-minded with its case for the therapeutic and moral potential of nature in the midst of the urban scene.

Sage initially thought that her planned community might provide housing for the working poor. But economic reality soon put paid to that. Instead, Frederick Law Olmsted Jr., the great park planner's son, was hired to lay out a garden community embodying Ebenezer Howard's belief in the restorative powers of trees and flowers on the work-exhausted white collar managerial class.

Adjacent to the Long Island Railroad, Forest Hills Gardens was to consist of a central common and some 1,500 houses on winding roads, the whole swaddled in greenery. The community officially opened in 1911, with an address by former President Theodore Roosevelt sonorously welcoming this fulfillment of the Progressive ideal of encasing nature's bounty in an urban setting.

Rounding out the vision, and nailing down the socioeconomic fact that this was not to be a lower-middle-class community, the West Side Tennis Club began its long residency in 1913. A decade later it added the stadium that made it the site of the tennis national championships. That lasted until the late 1970s, when the rise of Big Sports led to the opening of the National Tennis Center in nearby Flushing Meadows Park, the site of the 1939–40 and 1964 world's fairs.

So there was much history attached to the community into which we moved in the fall of 1941. But alas, it is of marginal relevance to the story I'm here to tell. What satisfaction my family and I derived from being able to say we lived in Forest Hills had no substantive connection to the Gardens and all it stood for.

Our Forest Hills had very different sources. One of these was the city-owned Independent (IND) subway line, which made central Queens accessible to Manhattan more rapidly and cheaply than the Long Island Railroad (LIRR). The subway reached Jamaica, the major Queens community beyond Forest Hills, in 1937. This enabled thousands of breadwinners like my father to contemplate a move to suburbia.

The other development that made it all possible was the New Deal's Federal Housing Authority. FHA mortgages, suitably protected against such dangers as African-American neighbors, replaced the old high-down payment, high-interest mortgages of the past with simple, inexpensive, government-insured instruments. The full consequences of this revolution in home financing and acquisition emerged in the explosion of car-driven suburbia during the postwar decades. But its character and social consequences were already evident in this prewar mini-diaspora, of which my family and I were a part.

Why did we move? The lure of home ownership is deep and well-nigh universal, and my family was hardly immune to it. I had a close friend from camp who had moved to Forest Hills in 1940, and I very much wanted to join him there. And I was twelve years old in 1941, close to high school. Forest Hills High School, which opened in early 1941, a few blocks from our new home, was touted as the crown jewel of the New York City secondary school system. Once again, family and social forces conjoined to set the course of my existence: my life as the product of my times.

New stand-alone houses, relatively substantial for the time, clustered around the high school. But they reached into the five figures: $10,000 to $11,000. A couple of blocks west, stretching in the direction of the socially unmentionable Italian-Irish working-class community of Corona, was a nondescript no-man's-land, already segmented into large blocks with sidewalks and sewers, ready for developers to develop. Here were built row houses costing $6,000 to $8,000, requiring down payments of $300 to $400 and monthly FHA-insured mortgage payments of $50 to $70.

This area lacked the graces of Forest Hills Gardens. The small-scale developers who put up our and our neighbors' houses did not have the clout (or the financial incentive) to indulge in real estate bells and whistles. Instead, the city bureaucracy labeled our area. Thus, 108th Street was the far-from-grand boulevard linking us to Forest Hills' main shopping drag, Austin Street, the LIRR, and the subway. Plots were reserved along 108th Street for apartment houses. Cord Meyer put up a few of them before 1941: all genteel extensions of the Gardens, all solidly closed to Jews. At right angles, between 108th and 110th streets, were the streets on which the row houses were built, their designations leagues away from the euphonious street names of the Gardens. My future wife's family moved to 108–45 65th Avenue in the fall of 1940; we came to grace 108–29 64th Road a year later. [Plate 10]

I suspect my father could have afforded one of the more upscale houses near the high school. But the newness of home ownership, and the familiarity with close-by neighbors engendered by decades of apartment living, proved to be decisive. (One gesture toward toniness: ours was only semi-attached, our side windows looking out on the non-majestic prospect of the driveway that allowed the street's homeowners' cars to make their way to their garages, a necessity even in pre-World War II row house suburbia. But, unusual among our neighbors, we were carless.)

So in we moved, and my father had to adapt to a classic commuter grind: a bus ride to cover the mile or so between our house and the subway, a forty-five-minute to one-hour subway ride, involving a transfer, to his place of work (Park Row, then Broadway) in lower Manhattan. But his self-employment allowed him to go in late and come back late, thus skipping the rush hour congestion that was just as real as—and could be even more unpleasant than—the traffic jams that already were a very visible part of suburban culture.

My mother's response to so substantial a relocation was to come down with pneumonia. As a twelve-year-old I was anxiously aware that she was in danger. But I was also in thrall to oncoming adolescence, heightened by the challenges and satisfactions of a new location. What to do with me on the weekends when I was around the house? Whenever possible, farm me out to family friends. Chief among these were Eliot and Mattie Fink. They had a daughter about my age. (I dimly recall some sexual fumblings, but nothing worth speaking of or remembering. I'm confident that my appeal, even to questing females of my age, was limited.)

Fink *père* was a window decorator, a step down the social-artistic ladder from my commercial artist father. And they were clearly below our family on the affluence scale. But they had social-climbing aspirations that matched my mother's more cultured yearnings. This led them to an apartment (in a building open to Jews) in tony Great Neck, further out on Long Island, just beyond New York City's *infra dig* identity. Close by the area enshrined in F. Scott Fitzgerald's *The Great Gatsby*, Great Neck had a *réclame* that put Forest Hills Gardens to shame. The Finks' flat, needless to say, was physically and socially as far from *that* Great Neck as we were from Forest Hills Gardens.

I vividly recall that on December 7, 1941, I was spending the day with the Finks in Great Neck. It was there that I heard the news of the Japanese attack on Pearl Harbor: a memory shared by every sentient American of the time. As a twelve-year-old I wasn't far enough into adolescence to indulge in enlistment fantasies. But I was old enough to be aware that I, and my time, had been catapulted into a historical event of world importance.

Even earlier, I had an awareness of war clouds gathering. I remember being sufficiently touched by the radio and newspaper furor over the 1937 Japanese attack on the American gunboat *Panay* on the Yangtze River to indulge in one of my periodic (and inevitably failed) attempts at model-making, using the bamboo-and-glue technique prevailing in those pre-plastic days.

Even more vivid is my recollection of being swept up, during the summer of 1940, in the Bundles for Britain furor of that tortured time, when England stood alone against Nazism. I do not, however, recall that my concern over the course of the war was shaped primarily by what was happening to Europe's Jews, one of the costs of my family's separation from the synagogue-going American Jewish community.

What was a pre-adolescent to do when confronting one of the great dramas in modern world history? Immerse himself in newspapers (ours—I can't imagine why—was the anti-New Deal *New York World-Telegram*), magazines (*Life* in particular), radio news, and movie newsreels. And draw maps. One wall of my not-too-ample bedroom was given over to as large a map of the world as I could fit in: my first (and last) artistic effort of any magnitude. My father, who I imagine was not happy over my manifest lack of the qualities necessary to go into the family business, derived some pride from this achievement, more notable for its size than its draftsmanship. On it I painstakingly water-colored in the territory lost or gained by the Allies. The ebb and flow in Russia led to a mix of colors that provided no indication whatever of who was up and who was down.

My war service consisted primarily of accompanying an air raid warden on (usually cold) autumn and winter nights to make sure that the streetlights were well and truly off, so that enemy bombers would not be able to strike our neighborhood. Just why the Germans might want to do so after coming all those thousands of miles is unclear—especially so since much of the surround consisted of empty lots frozen by the advent of war.

Otherwise, my contribution to the war effort centered on school. I faithfully pasted twenty-five-cent stamps in booklets which, when filled, got me a War Bond that in ten years would return twenty-five dollars, at a 2.9 percent interest rate. No Marxist dialectic of exploitation was at play here: eighty-five million Americans bought $185.7 billion worth of what were in effect below-market loans to the government. They served the dual purpose of helping to finance the war and siphoning off cash that otherwise might have fed inflation. Here, if I had the wit and the years to understand it, was a splendid instance of the new forces—of national identity and cohesion, of new resources (jobs, wages, profits) rapidly replacing the slack stagnation of the Depression—that were the first stages of a fundamental alteration of the country into which I had been born.

No less vivid (and no less ordinary) were other war-generated events that defined our days from December 1941 to August 1945. I entered Forest Hills High School in the fall of 1942, and very soon we gathered to mourn the first battlefield death of a graduate. There would be more. Otherwise, we filled our war bond books with stamps, collected metal trash, and were herded together for patriotic morale-boosters whose content quickly passed through us.

My war was in essence that of most of my generation, too young to fight but old enough to be aware of what was happening. We were the most direct beneficiaries of the Greatest Generation. We did not share in their sacrifices, but (at a remove) we were at one with them in perception and sentiment. This may explain why I (and others like me) never joined in the rejection of patriotism that swept over so many of the baby boomers in the 1960s and 1970s.

I have mixed feelings about the education I got—and eluded—during my Forest Hills years. In 1941 and 1942 I went to two elementary schools, moved about by a school administration trying to cope with the rising tide of new arrivals brought by the subway and the FHA. I began in P.S. 3, close by Forest Hills High School, a K-6 establishment stocked with kids from families like my own or higher up the socioeconomic ladder.

The only culturally discordant note was a group of kids—predominantly Italian and Irish—from a nearby orphanage: older, tougher, more resistant to what the school had to teach. Nevertheless, I don't recall any ugly physical encounters. The staff, I am sure, kept a wary eye on those outlanders. And the mores of the time worked against the anarchy that later came to afflict urban public schools.

No doubt reading, writing, and arithmetic were taught, and learned, there. But about all that I remember was an election for class president that I entered, driven by a pre-adolescent need to create a persona. My opponent was a much more personable fellow, to whom the prettiest girl in the class (my secret heart-throb) was attached. Shamefully, I won the election neither by program nor through personality, but by the promiscuous distribution of blotters inscribed with my name, secured by my father from an accommodating printer client. My opponent's inamorata burst into tears, thereby robbing the moment of what luster it might have had for me. I can't recall ever running for anything else, a judgment that stood me in good stead in ensuing years.

Occasionally my classmates and I were bused to P.S. 101 in Forest Hills Gardens, which was just about my only exposure to Old Forest Hills in these years. This was the consequence not of a burst of social engineering by the Board of Education bureaucracy but of P.S. 3's dearth of facilities. The boys were sent to learn the basics of carpentry (P.S. 101 had a workshop), the girls to learn the basics of cooking (it had a cooking classroom). Many of us, burdened with the primal Jewish curse of dextral clumsiness, were lucky to escape uncut or unburned. All I recall turning out were spectacularly misaligned bookends. Nor do I have the sense that my female counterparts moved rapidly from apple turnovers and brown Bettys to more savory culinary delights.

Perhaps this is why so many of my generation, as we rode the wave of mid-century, middle-class prosperity, devoted ourselves to hiring handymen and dining out.

After a brief stay in K-6 Elysium, many of us were sent to round out our primary education in the decidedly more downscale P.S. 14 in Corona. This was a social change of considerable magnitude. Corona was Irish, Italian, and working class; we were Jewish and middle class. Here was diversity with a vengeance. I had my share—more than my share—of one-sided (yours truly on the downside) fistic encounters with schoolmates generous in their dislike of Jews in general and me in particular. The teachers resented us as Jews, but were afraid of the fuss our parents were likely to raise if they physically disciplined us as they routinely did my Irish and Italian classmates. And they both resented and favored us as compliant, reasonably competent students. These facts, my being Jewish, and my lack of street-fighting smarts made me classic fair game for the townies. Given what we were (and were to be), and what they were (and were to be), it is hard to blame them.

Another chapter in this quotidian coming-of-age dramatically opened when I entered Forest Hills High School in 1942. The place was, by the city's standards, rather special. While not in the class of those jewels in the New York educational crown, Bronx Science, Stuyvesant, and Townsend Harris, FHHS gained luster from its shiny new plant and from its draw of middle class Jewish students whose parents were determinedly pushing them toward the professional/business world. (Half a century later this would be equally true of the Asian families flocking into my old neighborhood, one of whom bought our house.) FHHS was obligated to take all comers who resided within the catchment area of the surrounding neighborhood. The school also had a not-insignificant number of students from remoter areas of the City, who piggybacked on relatives' or friends' inside-the-area addresses to wiggle their way in.

FHHS's special cachet lay not in its building or its students, but in its teachers. A number were Jews who because of Depression-era poverty and anti-Semitism were unable to gain the advanced degrees or college appointments that were their due. The roll of honor included Wallace Mannheimer in math, Paul Brandwein in biology (who had a PhD and later became an important figure in science education), and Milton Zisowitz in English. (A favorite Mannheimer trick: he wrote a long series of numbers on the blackboard, faced away from them, and asked a student to name any three in succession. He then recited all that came before and after. The hook: they were the street numbers of the subway stations strung along the tortuous route from his Brooklyn home to City College, the goal of his daily commute.)

I was not well-suited to meet the intense, competitive work ethic of my more driven fellow students. This was due in part to the lack of strong family pressure to excel. While my mother did have aspirations for me, my father held them in lesser measure. Neither math nor science nor literature nor politics figured largely in our family's life. And there was the not-to-be-scoffed-at element of male adolescence, which did not foster a well-disciplined life of the mind.

So my grades in subjects that I did not naturally take to were, to put it politely, not top drawer. My mother was concerned enough to discuss with my father the prospect of sending me to Horace Mann-Lincoln School, a private school in Riverdale in the Bronx. The length of the commute and, I suspect, my father's reluctance to pay the tuition scotched the idea.

Arista, the school's honor society, was not for me. Among my blind spots: Latin, biology, and mathematics—except for geometry, which I found far more comprehensible than its chief competitor, algebra. In part this was due to a gifted instructor, Mannheimer; in part because (at least to me) geometry was less abstract than algebra. Apparently I was born with a taste for the material and concrete and a distaste for the theoretical and philosophical. It would, I see in retrospect, determine the kind of history I chose to do and how I went about doing it.

What I did achieve in an otherwise undistinguished high school career was to make a mark in writing. Under the goad of the delightfully acerb Milton Zisowitz, I began to write for the school newspaper and became one of a distended editorial board (including my future wife, of whose existence I was yet unaware). High school students, like soldiers and almost everyone else, were kept in line by the liberal distribution of honors: what the English accurately call Gongs.

In my senior year I had a burst of quasi-literary productivity and for the first time emerged from the undistinguished obscurity that until then characterized my high school career. Journalist-publicist Tex McCrary and actress-model Jinx Falkenburg got married in 1945 and became a pioneering glamour-celebrity couple in post-World War II New York. Not content with the Cafe Society life that then defined celebrity, they went on the radio in 1946 with one of the first talk shows, under the cutesy label of Hi Jinx. They broadcast, glamorously, from the top of the Empire State Building. But in those early days talk-show style was still embryonic. They were on at a decidedly non-glamorous early morning hour. And what to do on Saturday, when few citizens were up and fewer still were listening, was a problem.

Their early-days-of-talk-radio solution: assemble a board of high school editors, one from each borough, send them out on assignments, and have them report on the following Saturday program. At least the relatives and friends of the presenters might tune in. Forest Hills was the school of choice for Queens and I was its representative. This was heady stuff, and for perhaps the first time my parents had something to brag about.

It didn't last very long. I went on the program in the early spring of 1946 and graduated a few months later. Soon after that, Tex and Jinx ascended to increasing public celebrity as radio and then TV talk show hosts, at a more attractive hour and to a more substantial audience. The high school editor caper, I assume, quickly went into the dustbin.

Two moments in that brush with immortality do stand out. One of my assignments was to fly (fly!) down to Washington and interview General Lewis Hershey, director of the Selective Service System, a subject of considerable interest to high-schoolers and their parents in 1946. I don't remember what questions I posed to the general; I imagine that they were thoroughly callow and superficial. What I do remember was that when the interview drew to an end, Hershey asked me how old I was, and avuncularly assured me that I would soon be hearing from his operation.

Another spinoff of this breakout year was my emergence as a poet of sorts. In a burst of imitative creativity I wrote a Carl Sandburg-drenched poem about the city for an English class. My teacher, I imagine, was impressed by the fact that I knew enough to copy from Sandburg, and dispatched me to read my work at that year's inter-New York City high school poetry competition.

It was somewhere in Brooklyn, and I ambled into a room chockablock with the city's secondary school aesthetes. This, to put it mildly, was not my scene. But I read my work, and the judges (relatively high-powered: one of them was the actress Dorothy Stickney) must have been grateful for the respite that my devotedly derivative lines provided from the labored originality and high-flown sentience of my competitors. They gave me third prize, which enabled me to go up to a table displaying a variety of poetry books and select one from the residue left by the first and second prize winners. Quite out of my league (like that most favored person in the law, I was an innocent third party without notice), I chose by hefting the residue and taking the weightiest volume. As I recall, Ms. Stickney allowed herself a thin, ironic smile. I wound up with Louis Untermeyer's *Modern American Poetry*, which in coming years provided much pleasure and some knowledge of poetry to a culturally deprived youth.

News of my mini-triumph became public when the *New York Herald Tribune* printed a space-filler on the contest and its victors. Tex McCrary saw the item and asked me to read the poem on the following Saturday's program. (At the time, he was trying to induce his friend and client John Hay "Jock" Whitney to buy the newspaper; otherwise, I imagine, he did not follow the high school poetry scene.) And soon after that I got a prize (again, hardly a first prize) for the poem from *Scholastic Magazine*.

It would be nice to say that this was the beginning of a literary career. But I was far too callow, naïve, unformed, unconnected to anything beyond my not-very-intellectual middle class world to even imagine such a future. Instead I seized on a contest for high school essays proposing "A Food Plank for Peace." Why anyone would imagine that a New York City high school student had anything useful to offer on that subject beggars rational explanation. What did I know about food, beyond eating it? Still, this was a time of exceptional, and in retrospect exceptionally naïve, optimism. (We had just taken the leading role in establishing that archetype of postwar rationality and effectiveness, the United Nations.) I wound up as one of New York State's two winners, with a crack at the grand prize of a four-year college scholarship. Needless to say, I didn't win; I'm sure I came nowhere close.

The most important intellectual and cultural milieu during my high school years was (as it so often is) the mini-world that I and a coterie of friends made for ourselves. That was defined by the institutions and books best suited to appeal to what might clinically be described as smart-ass, not-very-intellectual New York Jewish teenagers. Sex figured, but not so prominently, I suspect, as it would have in later days. Taboos still were thick on the ground in middle-class boy-girl relationships, and even strait-laced "dates" were far more formal and rules-ridden than in the age of casual coupling to come.

Much of the ensuing libido suppression found release in humor. Laffmovie, a theatre devoted to comedies on the otherwise dirty-movie-laden Forty-second Street off Times Square, thoroughly schooled me and my buddies in the work of the Marx Brothers, the Three Stooges, and other masters of the genre. And when we weren't at Laffmovie, or that other form of popular postwar crafted entertainment, wrestling matches in Madison Square Garden, we read *The New Yorker* for its cartoons, Max Shulman's *Barefoot Boy with Cheek* for its often puerile humor, and, most of all, the writings of S.J. Perelman.

Perelman spoke to our taste for wordplay and punning and for the interaction of our immigrant Jewish roots with the lure of WASPy Anglo-American culture. We avidly shared his flights of verbal fantasy: ". . . with a blow I sent him groveling. In ten minutes he was back with a basket of appetizing fresh-picked grovels" or "Every man present [at a *soignée* Hollywood party] was, if not an Adonis, at least a Greek." We lapped up the cultural juxtaposition of Santa Claus and Jewish entrepreneurship in "Waiting for Santy," where S. Claus, a prominent bourgeois toy manufacturer, mistreats his worker gnomes. Chief among them is Rivkin, Communist and lover of Claus's daughter. When offered a piece of wax fruit by a co-worker, he reacts: "Imitations! Substitutes!" Thus we became aware of the presence of Clifford Odets (*Waiting for Lefty*) and of a world of Jewish radicalism alien to our suburban middle-class ambience.

And there was "Farewell, My Lovely Appetizer," which satirized the foibles of Raymond Chandler's tough detective Philip Marlowe ("I kicked open the bottom drawer of her desk, let two inches of rye trickle down my craw, kissed Birdie square on her lush, red mouth, and set fire to a cigarette.") All became part of the *lingua franca* of our teenage days.

We became ever deeper students of Perelman. We kept lists of words he used that we were unable to find in the dictionary. Once he gave a public lecture in Manhattan and one of our crowd went down to confront him with our list. He came back, sputtering with rage, and declared that the man was an idiot who had perfunctorily brushed aside the perfectly reasonable demand that he explain himself linguistically to a pimply adolescent. But our fandom also brought us (or at least me) an awareness that Perelman had a writer brother-in-law named Nathanael West, and thus led me to books that in the normal course of my teenage life I would not have encountered.

So, along with sandlot baseball and the other activities that kept boys of my age and station from straying off the bourgeois reservation, I began to camp out on the borderline of the life of the mind. By the time I finished high school, my career goal (insofar as I had one) was to be a reporter. That was reinforced by the fact that I had spent a couple of summers working for the *Forest Hills-Kew Gardens Post*, one of a string of struggling suburban sheets so short of staff that I wrote much of its content and made up the paper prior to its weekly publication. The most toothsome fringe benefit was a pass to the national tennis championships at Forest Hills' West Side Tennis Club. I enhanced what standing I had with my friends by entering through the gate and then, in an unobserved section of the fence that surrounded the stadium, transferring my pass to the next in line of my (at least for the moment) buddies.

This flurry of late-day mini-triumphs was capped by my winning a New York State Scholarship, whose $400 stipend went far to meet the tuition cost of most of the state's colleges. But I was hardly well-situated to enter what was at the time the quite novel struggle to gain admission to the school of one's choice (or at least not of one's non-choice). The flow of World War II veterans taking advantage of the GI Bill was at flood tide. The 1.5 million students in college in 1940 (16 percent of those who were eighteen to twenty-one years old) would be dwarfed by the 2.6 million (29 percent) by 1948. Colleges whose never-overlarge enrolments faded away during the war years suddenly had to cope with hordes of ex-GIs eager to get on with the opportunity of a post-secondary education provided by the GI Bill. The placid, sedentary pattern of previous college-going was turned upside down and inside out.

I had numerous deficits as I entered the swift-flowing stream of college admission-seeking. My grades and Regents scores (the tests that New York State administered to its high-schoolers) had a few alpine peaks, but broad and undistinguished lowlands:

good enough in normal times, but not in those fevered postwar days. Nor was my being Jewish any help at a time when the old anti-Semitism, though battered a bit by the war, was still alive and well in most college admissions offices. My rather thin list of other achievements was not likely to fare well against these obstacles.

So I struck out everywhere but at Queens College, my borough's branch of the municipal college system along with Brooklyn, Hunter, and the flagship City College of New York. My mother's delight at the prospect of my staying home was matched by my lack of delight at the prospect of my staying home. But there it was. Assuaged by the parental gift of a car (a 1939 Chevy Coupe Deville which made up by its sheer existence for the deficiencies that otherwise plagued it), I joined the otherwise overwhelmingly ex-GI Queens freshman class of 1946.

In many respects the transition from high school to college was seamless. My new institution resembled the one I had just left. Both were newly created; both were branches of the city's educational system; both catered heavily to the upwardly mobile Jewish population flowing into Queens; both were places you came to daily, but didn't live in.

My veteran-laden class could find comfort, too, in the familiarity of the Queens College plant: an old, turn-of-the-century set of buildings housing (not inappropriately) a boys' reform school, now supplemented by Quonset huts thrown up to handle the veteran flood, as was the case everywhere in collegeland. To add to the army camp atmosphere, retained articles of military dress were the prevailing fashion style of the ex-GI students. As the dominant majority, they shared a veteran culture from which we, the non-veteran minority, were excluded.

But despite these constraints—along with an indoor basketball court, on which we met our compulsory Phys Ed obligation, with a ceiling so low that the only viable set shot was one with the minimum geometrically possible parabola—it still was college. My first and, as it turned out, only year at Queens was most notable academically for a semester's exposure in the obligatory History of Western Civilization course to the teaching of J.H. Hexter, on his way to becoming one of the premier Tudor-Stuart historians of the Anglo-American historical world. A slight, ebullient, energetic fellow, Hexter had an infectious enthusiasm for history that lit a light bulb in my otherwise dim mental chandelier. My hazy career goal of being a journalist persisted, but now I began to find in history a subject that, if not the high road to riches, at least eased the path to an A.

My awareness of politics, such as it was, had been knee-jerk FDR/New Deal, as prevailing an attitude among my family, neighborhood, and friends as Republicanism would have been had I grown up in a small town in Kansas. This was an unreflective, low-key politics, not involved in the organizational intensity of Democratic Party affairs or the ideological rigors of the Marxist Left. Indeed, I was in retrospect remarkably insulated from the enthusiasms and excitements of the youthful Left, only mildly present in my relatively insulated suburban surround. My middle-middle class bourgeois world just wasn't susceptible to those fevers.

But Queens College was different. A number of my ex-GI classmates were more or less committed radicals of the Stalinist persuasion. However remote from the realities of life that history ultimately revealed them to be, these guys were a lot tougher than the typical adolescent play-Communists. Inevitably I was attracted by their worldly ways and other-worldly social ideals, though I have no memory of being drawn into the higher realms of party line-parsing, the favored form of commitment by those of my age and station.

I do recall a prototypical party member English instructor, who apparently mistook me for promising cannon fodder and invited me to a couple of soirees in his Greenwich Village pad. This was heady stuff indeed; and if I had stayed at Queens I might have swum further out into the cloudy waters of party activism and involvement.

I might have; but I doubt it. Neither family nor off-campus friends were into this world, and I had other things (history, tennis, girls—one girl in particular) to keep me engaged. And besides, after my freshman year my grades earned me admission to the University of Rochester. In so doing I made a definitive break from the Brooklyn-Forest Hills scene that had been my world through the Great Depression and World War II and, more definitively, from my childhood and adolescence.

CHAPTER THREE

Up and Out

T O LEAVE THE TIGHT LITTLE WORLD of Forest Hills and set off to Rochester and its university was, in a modest way, to share in the migratory experience of so many of my fellow citizens in the 1940s. Eleven million Americans served in the armed forces during the war. Millions more—most notably rural whites and blacks, and women—undertook no less traumatic migrations, social and economic as well as territorial, into the exploding world of wartime industrial production.

The slice of postwar America that I was entering differed in important respects from that larger scene. While higher education was expanding as never before, it still was little more than a blip on the American landscape. But in important respects it was a significant part of the new post-1945 American society emerging out of the generation-long crisis of the Depression and the war. As much as the suburban ranch houses, the ever more flamboyant cars, the baby boomer generation, and television (that as yet small storm cloud beginning to blot out the American cultural sun), the GI Bill-stoked, veteran-crammed postwar colleges were very much a part of where "it" (whatever "it" may have been) was.

My eight-hour train trip catapulted me not only into a new locale and a new educational setting, but into a world of people, ideas, and artifacts distant from anything that I had been accustomed to. One instance of this: The Eastman School of Music was a notable part of the University of Rochester, and several friends (and my roommate) were music students. In the spring of 1947 word circulated that a music store in town was touting a new kind of phonograph record. The hook: if you bought three of them, the store threw in a turntable. Not surprisingly, Rochester was a test town for the initial marketing of the long-playing record.

We rushed downtown to stock up on this new marvel. I stayed with standards (Brahms's *Second Symphony*, Beethoven's *Second* and *Seventh*). One of my more sophisticated musical friends went for relative esoterica such as Richard Strauss's *Death and Transfiguration*. A less serious member of our group responded to a playing of the piece: "My! That *is* a long-playing record."

Rochester was a good, and rich, university, at that time among the nation's best-endowed in terms of size. But it had no great social éclat—thank God. That made it much easier for a work in progress such as myself to gain entreé to a comfortable group of classmates with similar intellectual interests. Most of my closest friends were history majors. Socially we were a motley crew: second-generation Jews fresh from high school; veterans of middling origins, riding the GI Bill, better fixed on why they were there and where they were going than the rest of us; and a few upper-middle-class types at Rochester because they were from the area (a banker's son from Batavia) or because they couldn't get into a tonier college (the son of the editor of *Collier's*).

Much of my life at Rochester, as before, was resolutely unexceptional. I remained middle-tending-to-upper-middle class in the academic social hierarchy: good enough to get into the college's honors program, but nothing in my record (until my senior year) to catch anyone's attention. Much of my energy was devoted to my student coterie. In part this was because as an only child, limited in my teenage friendships, I reveled in a new world of college camaraderie. And in part it was because as a Jew I was barred from the non-Jewish fraternities that dominated campus social life, yet with my peculiarly non-Jewish upbringing did not feel drawn to the Jewish fraternity on campus.

The college life I experienced in the late 1940s was equidistant from once and future campus stereotypes. The WASPy, frat-and-football-colored world portrayed in the early-twentieth-century dime novels of Gilbert Patten about Frank Merriwell and in Owen Johnson's *Stover at Yale,* or in Hollywood's resolutely fictional campuses, was already fading into the past. Yet to arrive was the "liberated" college culture of the late twentieth century. In second-social-level Rochester, fraternity-sorority social preeminence and the importance of football struggled against a student body dominated by veterans drawn to the more sober business of making up for lost time and getting on with life.

I had my share of the old romantic view of college life. But it was a life from which I was effectively excluded by ethnicity and family upbringing. So I was drawn into a subset dominated by veterans well past the naiveté of the old college myth, a subset drawn as much as anything by the lure of an academic career.

Professorial life was not as yet defined by the perks of short semesters, low teaching loads, relatively good incomes, and removal from the market economy that attracted academic cannon fodder from the sixties on. I imagine that for some of my ex-GI friends, academia held out the promise of security and stability after a generation of depression and war. For a few of us who were younger (and Jewish), it in part spoke to an old ethnic tradition of bookishness and scholarship, devalued by the rigors of immigration and hard times but now given new credence and value by the turn against anti-Semitism in the wake of World War II and the Holocaust. And at least for me there must have been a whiff of the aura of heightened social status (if not economic class) attached to the ivory tower.

In the course of my undergraduate years I came increasingly under the sway of fellow students and faculty who in their different ways identified with the attractions of the academic life. My initial interest in journalism gave way to the lure of history graduate school.

Why history? Because, first, it elicited a more engaged (and successful) intellectual and academic response from me than did any other subject. To have grown up in the 1930s and 1940s was a powerful incentive to want to find out why the Depression and the War had happened. Less elevated (but perhaps more decisive in my case) was the aura of social identification with Old America attached to the study of the nation's past. (The still-higher place on the academic pecking order of medieval or renaissance, or cultural or intellectual, history was beyond my limited stage of status consciousness.)

And—I think decisively—the Rochester History Department, in particular its American wing, was unusually good, and engaged, and interested in undergraduates. It included, in my time there, Glyndon Van Deusen, who wrote influential biographies of Martin Van Buren, Thurlow Weed, and Horace Greeley; the then-young Richard Wade, who went on to be a major urban historian; and, looming over the department (in physical as well as reputational stature), Dexter Perkins, who wrote more volumes on the history of the Monroe Doctrine than anyone had ever done before, or ever would again.

What made the difference, I think, was Perkins' unusual persona and the stylistic stamp that he put on the department. He had strong New England Brahmin roots; his aunt was Fannie Farmer of cookbook fame, then edited by his wife, Wilma. He lived in a substantial house on the city's most fashionable street, East Avenue. Most of all, he was secure enough in his sense of himself—as a person, as a historian—not to be soured by his failure to have an Ivy League professorship. Instead he committed himself wholeheartedly to his second-level institution, and brought more than a touch of the best Brahmin style to western New York. Through seminars and dinners at his home and meetings with visiting scholars (I remember a descent by Yale's chauvinistic diplomatic historian Samuel Flagg Bemis, whom Dexter mischievously introduced as Samuel Wave-the-Flag Bemis), he introduced callow undergraduates such as myself to what the academic life might be.

So comfortable in his own skin was Dexter that he transcended the anti-Semitism that then was the mothers' milk of academics, not least historians. I vividly recall running into him on campus in the spring of my senior year (not literally: to have done so, given his ample frame, would have been to sustain substantial personal injury). "What are you planning to do when you graduate, Mickey?" he asked in his piping, Brahmin-Boston voice. (His diction could be delightfully idiosyncratic. He once announced in class: "isolation [the "i" pronounced as in "idiocy"] is idiocy [the "i" pronounced as in "isolation"]. I told him that I had given up my interest in journalism, and intended to go to history graduate school. "That's wonderful! It's very difficult for a Jew in history, but I'll do everything I can to help you. Where do you intend to go?" I told him that I was thinking of Princeton. (Several young faculty members had been touting the place to me; I had visited it and had a conversation with medievalist Joseph Strayer, whose substance, mercifully, I can't recall: it's hard to imagine what we had to say to each other.) Dexter airily brushed this aside: "You don't have to worry about that. I guarantee I'll get you into Harvard." (And so, eventually, he did.)

It helped that I finally raised my rather torpid academic performance level at the end of my senior year. I spent my junior and senior years in Rochester's honors program, a knockoff of the Swarthmore seminar system, in which a chosen few took two seminars a semester during their last two years, usually writing a paper a week in each seminar. (I'm not sure how much—or if—Dexter read our efforts in his seminar, which I imagine demonstrated conclusively that it is possible to do sophomoric work in one's junior and senior years. Nevertheless, our desire to put on a show led to our grinding out twenty-five-page to thirty-page tomes every other week.)

The two years of seminars culminated in a big end-of-senior-year blowout, in which outside examiners administered written exams and followed them up with oral grillings. They then determined the kind of degree—summa, magna, honors, or pass—that each of us would get.

Going into this extravaganza, my junior year performance suggested something at best in the honors/high honors range. I set myself the goal of two highest and two highs in my senior exams, thus locking in a high honors (magna) degree. I announced as much in a banner suspended over my desk. That was not, apparently, a sufficient goad to excel. I had not had anything like, say, a late twentieth-century South Korean student's family schooling in career discipline, and I continued to go off to what I fondly thought of as dissolute evenings (martinis, shrimp cocktails, not-very-original explorations of the Meaning of Life): burning the midnight vapors instead of burning the midnight oil. My long-suffering roommate finally had enough, and during one of my absences modified my goad-banner to a much more modest three passes and one honors.

As it happened, I had a couple of good days in the exam-and-interview process (simpatico questions, examiners unaware of my checkered undergraduate past). I got enough highest honors grades to just scrape into the range of eligibility for a summa degree, and they gave it to me. It is hard to know who was more outraged by this injustice: the other summa designees (who had earned their distinction the hard way) or the Rochester history faculty, who had a more informed sense of my undergraduate record. In any event, Harvard let me know in the summer that it was reversing an earlier rejection: "Application reconsidered in light of further information."

I tell this story at inordinate length because it was important in my life (though not to my times), and because it suggests that, the cliché to the contrary notwithstanding, there *can* be a second act in American life. Indeed, to get somewhere from nowhere is as American as you can be.

And so in the fall of 1950 I set out for Harvard and yet another abrupt and substantial change of scene. Before doing so, my father gave me a summer trip to Europe. The war was five years past. (It was just about then that a Harvard alum observed that not having gone to Harvard was like not having gone to Europe.) So off I went aboard the Holland-America Line's old *S.S. Volendam* (New York to Plymouth in a brisk ten days) along with hundreds of other youths more or less indistinguishable from one another.

I find travel accounts, unless they are exceptionally insightful or artistic, to be crashing bores, and will spare you mine—with two exceptions.

I arrived in England in June 1950. A friend had secured tickets to Parliament. As it happened we went on the day when Prime Minister Clement Attlee and former Prime Minister Winston Churchill spoke on the just-ignited Korean War. Neither what they said or what I made of it was of any great significance, nor remains in my memory. But in retrospect I suppose that being an eyewitness to history (however attenuated) reinforced me in my belief that what I was intending to do with my life was worth doing.

Along the same line: on July 4, ever on the qui vive for free grub in my just-out-of-college way, I hied myself to the American Embassy's Independence Day bash. (Tourism was still small enough to let them throw open the gates.) It was a reassuringly American moment: loud, bumptious, boisterous; no noticeable style or grace; no obvious concern for British sensitivities in its unrestrained celebration of the break from Perfidious Albion; the larger purpose of commemoration buried somewhere under a mountain of food and drink (at a time when rationing was still the rule in England).

In due course I emerged from this Lucullan—or better, Bacchanalian—scene. Down the street was an orphanage, or some such place, celebrating the opening of a new wing, or some such thing. A large Daimler-like limousine (upon reflection, I conclude that it *was* a Daimler) pulled up, and out came a personage recognizably the Queen Mother. She swept in to perform her royal duties with what I remember was magnificent disregard for the Yankee boisterousness nearby. That (along with the salutation from a French *flic* on my first day in Paris, when I engaged in a quite normal New York jaywalk—"Espèce de chien!") brought home, as no reading could, that we may be one humanity, but we do march to different drummers.

Otherwise I coasted along the traditional tourist high spots: not a Grand Tour, but in those strong-dollar, thank-you-for-the-Marshall-Plan days, not a De-Tour either. I did get to see Soviet-occupied Vienna and the (cleared but not yet rebuilt) bomb sites of London. I met a few Holocaust survivors (relatives of a shipboard acquaintance) but without as yet having any full sense of how that event affected me as a Jew.

After this minor-league rite of passage, I made my way to Cambridge, Massachusetts, and the peculiar form of experience—part penal, part liberating—that graduate school can be. In many respects being a history graduate student at Harvard in the early 1950s was not hugely different from being an undergraduate at Rochester in the late 1940s—except that I got more personal instruction, though perhaps less intellectual stimulation, at Rochester. [Plate 11]

Part of this aridity stemmed from a still-veteran-crowded student body (though less so than in college a few years before). But most of it reflected the prevailing view of graduate education in history at Harvard then, a view not unlike that of Spartan child-rearing in the fifth century BC. Those perceived as gifted (in this case as potentially notable historians, not potentially savage warriors) were to be nurtured and fostered. The others, if not to be exposed to wild animals and the elements as in the case of many Spartan female infants, were left to shift more or less for themselves.

Like a Spartan upbringing, this made some sense. To be a historian is, more than in most occupations, to be a loner. After all, reading (which is what we did, and did, and did) is a good way of meeting the (Chico) Marxian challenge: "Who you gonna believe? Me or your own eyes?" It is, or should be, deeply written into historians' DNA to choose the latter, not the former. But being part human, many fail to do so, which is why so much guff gets passed off under Clio's imprimatur.

Still, life alone on the Harvard cliff's edge could get dicey. I took a couple of courses in American colonial history with Samuel Eliot Morison, the preeminent figure in the field. Morison's Brahmin credentials were impeccable, but his Brahmin capital was less so. Like Churchill, he made up for his fiscal shortfall by his writing, and compensated for any accompanying social sensitivity by an *echt*-Brahmin lifestyle.

His classes in colonial history were social more than intellectual revelations to this unwashed (though wet behind the ears) participant. He started us off with a solid month on Columbus's voyages, his specialty, the more-than-you-want-to-know details leavened by his frequent appearances in riding habit and boots, fresh from a morning canter, and his not infrequent expulsion of undergraduates who had the affrontery to appear in the obligatory jacket but without the obligatory tie.

After our immersion in Columbusiana, Morison graciously gave us an hour to ask questions. In response to one of them, he observed *en passant* that scurvy didn't appear in transatlantic voyages until well into the sixteenth century. An undergraduate (no graduate student would have had the necessary self-assurance) interjected: "But sir: Columbus's men had scurvy." Patrician eyebrows went up; the silence was prolonged. Then: "Thank you. I didn't know that."

Even my grad-student, not-planning-to-do-colonial-history anonymity did not shield me from this Brahmin hauteur. I wrote a paper on South Carolinian Henry Laurens, a president of the Continental Congress about whom I knew little and cared less. (Why did I write on Laurens? I could well have been assigned to do it.) In a misjudged act of academic showmanship, I concluded with the observation that, for all his relative inconsequence, Laurens deserved a better fate than not even being mentioned in Edward Channing's *A History of the United States.* I didn't know that Channing was Morison's revered teacher. In his comment on the paper he informed me that the reason Channing ignored Laurens was that the standard biography of the South Carolinian had not yet appeared. (I still don't think that was much of an explanation.) He, Morison, had Channing's copy of that biography, and if I ever published anything on Laurens, he would give it to me.

I wasn't sufficiently in Morison's orbit to be upset. But another, even more hayseedy fellow graduate student did have his sights set on colonial history. Imagine how he felt when Morison invited him to dinner. Then imagine how he felt when, afterward, Morison took him to his study and instructed him on how he had to cast off his Kansas ways if he wished to succeed at Harvard.

A final touch of Morisoniana: while frantically swotting for my general examination, I realized that I knew almost nothing about colonial American literature. That seemed like a good excuse to visit Morison, who would be grilling me in that field, ask for his advice, and create in him some awareness of my existence. I summoned up the courage to enter his Widener Library sanctum and ask if there was anything else I should read besides

Moses Coit Tyler's history of colonial literature, the one authority on the subject of whose existence I was aware. "Tyler!" he exclaimed, looking straight through me to broader fields beyond. "I must include him in the *Harvard Guide* [*to American History*, then under way]." He made an appropriate note to himself, and then turned to other things, seemingly oblivious to my presence. I slipped out, cut down to a size two.

No less distant from today's more easygoing academic world was my experience in Arthur Schlesinger Sr.'s seminar in American social history. Today that subject is awash in race-class-gender concerns. Not then. Schlesinger handed out a list of subjects having to do with that year's decade of choice, the 1880s. Drawing on my past interest in journalism, I selected the topic of Joseph Pulitzer's impact on New York journalism. This came down to measuring the column inches of Pulitzer's *World* and several pre-existing New York dailies over the course of the 1880s with a view to seeing how various categories (crime, sports, foreign news, politics) changed under the impact of the interloper.

In those pre-computer days, my research design consisted of endless hours with a ruler, a pencil, and a pad of paper. I turned in a 120-page-plus paper in which I conclusively demonstrated that Joseph Pultizer's arrival on the New York newspaper scene had diverse and varied consequences. Schlesinger had no adverse reaction to the puerility of my results. But he did check my first twenty-five footnotes, and found that in one case I had transcribed "to-day" as "today," and in the other had committed an error of comparable magnitude. His comment: "My checking of your footnotes was not very reassuring."

Spartan, indeed. I suppose it did instill in me a lifelong duty of care when it came to research; but at what cost in the joy of finding, and saying, something new about the past?

That came, instead, in my other first-year seminar, with Oscar Handlin. He and Arthur Schlesinger Jr. were the tenured post–World War II additions to Harvard's American history faculty. Handlin's *The Uprooted* would win the Pulitzer Prize in History in the spring of 1952. But I drifted into auditing his course in immigration history the previous fall, presumably responding to scuttlebutt that something new and exciting was going on there (and perhaps to a visceral sense that immigration history was, in part, mine own).

There were twenty-odd students (minute by Harvard standards) in Handlin's class. We were subjected to a hesitant, uninflected style of lecturing (long pauses while he sought just the right word) that was tortuously frustrating even to so deferential a crowd as circa 1950 Harvard undergraduates. But I found his subtle, sophisticated analysis of how American history played out an entirely new and wholly exciting way of looking at the past.

So I became a Handlin student (to Schlesinger Sr.'s manifest displeasure; Dexter Perkins had told me to work with him, and so informed his friend, and Schlesinger apparently thought my seminar paper acceptable despite its transcription errors). My ex-GI fellow students were in a hurry to get through graduate school in order to make up for time lost. I was in no less of a rush, but for the opposite reason: to get as much of the PhD program under my belt as quickly as possible before the obligation to do my bit in the Korean War beckoned. In that sense, history was as much a reality for me as it was for my World War II–blooded contemporaries.

When I entered Harvard in the fall of 1950, the Korean War was well into its depressing early stage, and I had to get year-by-year deferments from my draft board. By early 1953 the board was getting antsy and my wife was expecting a baby in September. The logistical and financial prospects of being drafted were not attractive, so I decided to try to be a Naval intelligence officer. I managed, in the spring of 1953, to squeak through the eye examination and was accepted for the officer candidate program, which involved a bracing three months in Officer Candidate School at Newport, Rhode Island, and then a not-so-bracing three years of active duty.

The ink was barely dry on my enlistment papers when a new policy of exempting fathers was promulgated and the Korean War entered into its mummified state of armistice. So as it turned out, I needn't have gone into military service.

How did I then feel about this turn of fortune's screw? How have I felt about it since? The answer underlines, as few other things can, how different was the world view of those of us who were shaped by the Great Depression and/or the Second World War from those shaped by the 1960s, the Vietnam War, and after.

I remember being disappointed, of course, but also attracted by the prospect of echoing, however imperfectly, the experience of the veterans I had gone to school with, of being part of something larger: an important national experience. That attitude would be all but incomprehensible to baby boomers and their successors. To meet the demands of citizenship in this way was, for most of them, the precise opposite of my mindset. Many of them devoted themselves not only to escaping military service, but to actively resisting it. The draft in my time was already a creaking, decreasingly supported national policy; after its disastrous impact in the Vietnam War the nation got rid of it in 1973. Registration was restored in 1980, but not conscription.

A skeptical, at times cynical, view of military service in my time was, I think, evident more among working class than affluent and educated Americans. The implication and significance of World War II, and even the cold war, was much more a part of the world view of the educated and the better-off. Now that is gone, or reversed. It is difficult to imagine an American military venture, however justifiable its source, that would not be rejected now by the *jeunesse doré* and the chattering classes.

Going off to fight (or, more accurately, to listen in on) the Soviets and the Chinese was to some degree like the prospect of being hanged: it spurred me to get on with my current agenda. I took my general examination, the first major challenge on the road to a PhD, near the end of my second year in graduate school, instead of, as was customary among my peers, in my third year. I was also pushed to this by my advisor Oscar Handlin, who shortly before *der Tag* told me that it was obligatory for me to take the exam when I did. I asked him why this was the case, since none of my contemporaries was doing so. He replied that it was because I had gotten an MA degree at Rochester. I pointed that I had done no such thing. He seemed surprised, but bore the news with far more equanimity than I did.

The general examination was like most of what one did to get a PhD: fulfilling requirements that (perhaps appropriately in a history program) had the musty air of customs long adhered to but with no updated sense of their relevance. Thus examiner Samuel Eliot Morison, who appears to have been resigned to the accelerating entry of unwashed (and decreasingly uncircumcised) newcomers, had what might be charitably called a disinterested view of the proceedings. "Mr. Keller," I recall him asking, "describe St. Brendan's Isles." "But sir," I replied, "they were imaginary." "I know that," he irritably declared. "What did explorers of the time *think* they looked like?" What could the man be looking for? Since I couldn't figure *that* one out, I decided to play it straight: "They thought there were seven isles, stretching from northwest to southeast." "Precisely," he replied, clearly deciding that someone so learned might not, after all, be a detriment to the profession.

Even before I got through my general examination, I was at work on my thesis. In part this was because, with the military looming over me, I was in a hurry. Also in part (perhaps because I was down in the departmental account book as a journeyman and not a star), because I was presented with a topic, and most of the necessary primary sources, on a silver (plated) platter. Handlin called me in one day to tell me that the son of James Montgomery Beck wanted someone to write a biography of his father and would make the Beck Papers available for the author's private use.

The subject had been a corporation lawyer, solicitor general in the 1920s, a far-from-distinguished congressman, and a prominent critic of the New Deal: hardly a stirring resume. But in a sense I was ready for the topic. From my college days on, I had an interest in A. Mitchell Palmer, President Woodrow Wilson's attorney general toward the end of his presidency and enshrined in history for the infamous raids—the Palmer Raids— that in early 1919 swept up hundreds of aliens with radical or revolutionary inclinations. What drew me to so unsavory a character? Even now, I have no real idea. Perhaps the fact that he was often mentioned in books and lectures, yet remained (not surprisingly) biography-less, attracted me. It is hard to see any more profound reason. I was neither sufficiently on the Right to be sympathetic toward the man, nor Left enough to want to use him as the embodiment of a reactionary society.

So I took the bait. I worked on the papers in Beck Jr.'s Park Avenue apartment during the summer of 1951. Then the papers were deposited temporarily in Harvard's Houghton Library (eventually they went to Beck Jr.'s alma mater, Princeton), and I had permission to work with them in my apartment. (Sam Morison had done *his* dissertation, on his ancestor Harrison Gray Otis, using papers deposited in a relative's home. The difference in the social and cultural contexts of these two home-bound projects nicely sums up the gulf between Morison's world and mine.)

My Harvard sojourn turned out to be, by PhD standards, a brief one: three years. In spirit and through experience I remained close to the ex-GI generation that so influenced me in my college years. My life agenda, too, was shaped by the imposition of military service; and like them, I was spurred by the sense of a need to make up for lost time. My early general exam allowed me to spend my final, pre-Navy year as a graduate student working in relevant manuscript collections at the Library of Congress and elsewhere and to get going on a first draft of my thesis.

After a consuming three months at Officer Candidate School in Newport, in the fall of 1953 I was assigned to the Naval Security Station on Nebraska Avenue in northwest Washington, where then abided the highly secret National Security Agency, which handled the Navy's cryptography—message-intercepting-and-decoding—mission. [Plate 12]

Since I was both mathematically and linguistically challenged, I had little in the way of special talent to offer. While the powers that be sorted out what to do with me, I served as officer of the day (and night) on staggered eight-hour shifts and got a rudimentary education in overseeing the work of receiving, sending, and decoding that the Navy's Communications Intelligence (COMINT) branch was charged to do.

This was neither intellectually nor time-demanding. In the ebb tide of the Korean War, the tropistic inclination of the military bureaucracy to make-work flourished luxuriantly. So I had much opportunity (and considerable motivation, given the increasingly clear message that I had made a large career mistake in joining up) to continue to work on my dissertation.

After a few months in Washington, with our first-born daughter an additional spur to my sense that I had best get on with things, I was given that not-so-common offer in military life: a choice of assignments. I could go out (for a year by myself, or for a year and a half with my family) to serve in the Communications Intelligence station in either the mid-Pacific island of Guam or the Aleutian island of Adak. We settled on remote, wind-ridden Adak rather than remote, heat- and insect-ridden Guam. Why? Some atavistic Jewish distaste for the corrupt(ing) tropics, perhaps?

In any event, I emplaned to Adak via Seattle, where I had to wait for several days until the weather allowed a plane to get to Anchorage. Then, after an extended layover in Anchorage until a plane had a reasonable chance of landing, I made it to Adak. Climate as well as geography conveyed the same message: you, my lad, are on your way to a powerful claimant to the end of the earth.

After a couple of months my wife and daughter joined me, after a journey beset by unsympathetic airline hostesses and accommodations for our baby at a Kodiak Island layover sufficiently conducive to crib death to encourage my wife to spend the night watching over her.

Despite all this, neither of us fell prey to depression. We were young; we were naïve culturally, with little sense that we were missing a great deal by tending to an infant on Adak rather than in some more salubrious setting. Our housing was good; there were others of our age and condition among the other officers. (We were socially and residentially segregated from the enlisted men). Most of all, the demands of a still-young marriage and a still-infant daughter enmeshed us in a life in which the surround was of reduced consequence.

So we made our way as best we could. A big event was the monthly appearance of a supply ship which brought fresh lettuce, ice cream, and other rarities—along with a supply of books for my dissertation requisitioned from the Oregon State Library. Recollecting in tranquility, I am struck more by the relevance of the cliché that our marriage, our character, and my fortitude (and perhaps my insight) as a historian were strengthened by these rigors, than by the alternative cliché that our lives and my career were blighted by physical and cultural deprivation.

All I know is that after a year-plus on Adak, we returned to a final Navy year in Washington, not greatly changed and as far as I can recall not emotionally or socially diminished by our Aleutian idyll. Indeed, I would argue that the experience deepened my determination to get on with the business of my life: a social attitude that was widely shared by ex-GI graduate students, though perhaps not so much by my contemporaries, who remained in Cambridge to savor the delights of tutorships and the life of the (Harvard) mind.

One measure of this: I managed to complete my dissertation, defend it, and get my PhD while I was still in the service. (I finished the first draft while in Adak, and hot-footed to the post office to send it off to my advisor Handlin, who at the time was on sabbatical in Switzerland. The logistics of sending a package from Adak to Switzerland had an impact on the face of the gob at the Navy Post Office that still is vivid in my mind's eye.)

I defended my dissertation in the spring of 1956, back in Washington for my final Navy year. To prepare myself, I took two weeks' leave and dug into the American history holdings of American University in Washington, across the street from the Naval Security Station where I was assigned. In those simpler days, the collection fit into one room, so all I had to do was— literally—read around. Harriet Dorman, History's longtime secretary and the departmental conscience, coldly informed me when I came to Cambridge for my dissertation defense that this was the first time in *her* experience that a graduate student got his degree while still in the military. I didn't have the wit to reply that if the Korean War had still been on, I was confident that this unthinkable event would not have happened; but in fact the war was not on, but off.

So as my Navy term ran out in the summer of 1956, my wife, two children now, and I faced yet another big turn in the world we inhabited. By this time the depression in faculty hiring that came with the cessation of the GI intake and the falloff of student enrollment during the Korean War was coming to an end. Jobs were not yet as plentiful as they would be in years to come, but they were by no means rare.

I was not a hot property. My three years as a graduate student at Harvard (much of it caught up in family affairs and frantic study and research before entering the Navy) did little to school me in the academic arts. I had a working knowledge of professorspeak, but could hardly claim to be fluent in the patois. This became evident when I came to bat, and struck out, in interviews at Wesleyan and Amherst. (I was hardly thought fit, by those who managed these things, to be sent off to interviews at major research universities.)

Pressured by the need to be earning (rather than learning) a living after I left the Navy in the summer of 1956, I moved a notch or two down the academic pecking order. I recall a bizarre interview (I am sure that I was as bizarre to my inquisitors as they were to me) at St. John's College at Annapolis, Maryland. This survival of the Hutchins-Adler dream of an education defined by Great Books and Outmoded Science was hardly a good fit for a narrowly professional Harvard PhD. The faculty search committee proposed that I teach elementary biology and music appreciation along with presumably more appropriate courses in literature, history, and philosophy. This, to under-state, was not what I had set out, and been prepared, to do.

I gave some brief thought to applying to the intelligence branch of the State Department, but quickly abandoned what would have been a disastrous mismatch: bureaucratic-administrative skill was not at the top of my personal pecking order. Then, some light in the tunnel. The University of North Carolina at Chapel Hill imposed a standardized course in the History of the West on its massive freshman intake, overseen by the History Department but staffed by a separate Social Science staff. In those days, most state universities took any student who met the far-from-onerous entrance requirements, and depended on the freshman courses to cull the herd numerically and qualitatively: euthanasia rather than birth control, in the unfeeling expression of the time.

Clearly the need for warm bodies to tutor these multitudes was great. And a Harvard PhD looked good. So I was hired over the phone. Soon after my departure from the Navy, my family and I took up what turned out to be not-so-new a life in Chapel Hill.

I had a profession—college teaching—to learn. I did so through the academic equivalent of being tossed into the water and left to swim or drown. I started out by teaching four sections of the Western Civilization course, each of which met three times a week. Only three preparations a week were required. But this added up to four hours a day, six days a week, of classes, starting at 8 a.m.—by academic standards, the equivalent of a stint in a Siberian salt mine. After a year of such sweated labor, I was given the privilege of teaching a couple of sections of the American History survey course, another mass-production offering.

We lived in a garden apartment complex much like the one we inhabited in Falls Church, Virginia, during my Navy days. Similarly situated young families abounded here as there and determined much of our social life. One (non-Southern) history professor, Frank Klingberg, was notably welcoming; most of my other colleagues less so. This was something we didn't notice until, after two years in Chapel Hill, on the evening before our departure for Philadelphia and a position at the University of Pennsylvania, a colleague paid us a visit and stayed into the small hours of the morning telling us of our impact on the Department of History.

It turned out that not until I arrived on the scene was it realized that I was a Jew: the department's first. One senior historian, ever-ready to build on his substantial hostility to blacks, refused to have us to his house for dinner, an assertion of principle whose impact was diluted by our blissful unawareness of its existence.

To be teaching in Chapel Hill in the late 1950s was to be enmeshed willy-nilly in the gathering civil rights revolution. In our politically and socially unsophisticated liberal way, we tried to do our part. I volunteered to teach an American History survey course at North Carolina College, the state system's all but all-black branch in Durham. That gave me direct exposure to what segregation could do to the education and self-esteem of its victims.

My wife involved herself in a right-minded fight to integrate a planned public library, Chapel Hill's first. This, like so much of the town, was closed to blacks. In the spirit of the separate-but-equal policy of the time, a reading room of sorts was to be set up in the community center of Carrboro, Chapel Hill's adjacent black ghetto. In a particularly evocative instance of separate-but-equal at play, this contribution to intellectual advancement was to be located in the center's ping-pong room.

These activities were hardly in the class of a summer of voter organizing in Mississippi. And Chapel Hill was widely regarded as one of the South's more liberal communities. Indeed, some of our local white friends who cared about the issue of race were among the most admirable people I have ever met. They effectively made it impossible for me to respond warmly to the visceral anti-Southern bias of the Northern liberal *unco guid* so thick on the ground in the Northern University world in which we spent the rest of our lives.

But Chapel Hill's enlightenment did not extend to allowing blacks to patronize the town's drug store. And a physically segregated section of the UNC football stadium, directly facing the setting sun, was where blacks were allowed to cheer on the (all-white) football team of the (all-white) university.

In that time and place, even moderately liberal Southern friends could not easily repudiate their ties to the Southern past. On the eve of our departure from Chapel Hill, one of them gave us a handsome set of George Bancroft's *History of the United States*. His inscription: "Sherman's men took our other set. You might as well have this one."

CHAPTER FOUR

Riding the Wave

I WAS DESTINED to ride the wave of social change that transformed higher education and, indeed, American life in general during the second half of the twentieth century. My dissertation, rewritten to free it from some of the constraints on readability imposed by the conventions of the PhD, was accepted for publication by Coward-McCann, a trade publisher. Its readiness to do this was stoked by a subvention from the subject's son. In those simpler days, my book garnered a review by Columbia historian John Garraty in the *New York Times Book Review*. It was favorable, but its utility was diminished by the review appearing coincidently with a New York newspaper strike that prevented anyone from seeing it. When the strike ended some time later, it was reprinted along with other missing-in-action casualties, so it had the rare distinction of being unread twice.

But the book did up my ante in what was rapidly becoming a seller's market for academic positions. Offers came in from Washington University's History Department, now presided over by my old Queens College professor J.H. Hexter, and from the University of Pennsylvania. The latter was part of the Ivy League and closer to family, so this was not a difficult choice.

Off we went in the summer of 1958 to replay, once again, our recurrent family scenario of picking up old stakes and setting down new ones. When we finally, and permanently, settled in Cambridge in 1964 it was our thirteenth change of abode in the eleven years of our marriage: not unique in an age of military service and high geographical mobility.

We were enamored, as were so many of our generation, by the lure of the suburbs. We spent our Navy and Chapel Hill years in garden apartment complexes. And our peripatetic life left us immune to the urban-bohemian value system of my more *soignée* fellow-academics. That, and the presence of two small children, meant that we gave not a moment's thought to Center City Philadelphia, still in the 1950s urban doldrums, or West Philadelphia adjacent to the Penn campus. The latter was an East Coast version of Hyde Park (not least for its high crime rate), but without the intellectual gravitational pull of the University of Chicago.

We found an attractive piece of land overlooking virginal Ridley Creek in the idyllic-looking "community or populated place" of Moylan, a political subdivision of Nether Providence Township a couple of miles west of Swarthmore. This exurban utopia rested on a commuter rail line that swept me into Philadelphia's Thirtieth Street station, a short walk to the Penn campus.

Our social naiveté did not extend to the regnant suburban split-level architectural traditionalism. Instead we put up a Techbuilt, a contemporary prefab designed by Walter Gropius disciple Carl Koch. Redwood siding and its striking view over a picturesque creek valley, farmland, an eighteenth-century farmhouse, and a Pennsylvania Dutch barn did not fully erase the house's production-line lineage. We proudly displayed our residence to a visitor, who exclaimed: "Why, it's a Techbuilt! My sister has two of them."

It's a rare paradise that is wholly paradisaical. In the adjacent upscale borough of Rose Valley, full of high-end professionals and academics, there was a community center with a pool, a near-necessity for a family with small children during a hot Philadelphia summer. But it emerged that until recently Rose Valley had been run by a *Gauleiter* who had been a member of the pro-Nazi Silver Shirts, and it still enforced a ukase that kept Jews out of the pool. (This may have been a factor in the decision of future Nobelist economist Simon Kuznets, who lived in Rose Valley in the 1940s, to leave Penn.) The exclusion was still in effect when we arrived. A right-thinking Quaker neighbor came by and offered to join us in making a cause celebre of the rule. But meanwhile we had found a pool with a more open attitude in a nearby township, and decided not to fight the good fight. It is a decision that I regret to this day.

We discovered also that not all Quakers fit the liberal stereotype. Our neck of the Philadelphia suburban woods had a number of birthright Quaker families who, generation after generation, went to Westtown School in nearby West Chester or the Friends' schools in Philadelphia, and then to Haverford, Swarthmore, or Bryn Mawr. This vigorous parochialism, given the fervid geographical mobility of Americans in the fifties, was almost . . . un-American. Certainly it bred hostility to Outsiders, which we most certainly were. A swastika appeared one day on our toolshed, and we began to think that Quaker benevolence stood in inverse relation to the nearness of the object of its benevolence.

Now I was a full-fledged member of a substantial History Department. But the academy, no less than residential communities, was still in the process of sloughing off old ways, old prejudices. I was the first Jewish appointee in American history at Penn. (A self-effacing colleague in Renaissance history had previously breached the line.) There was as yet no faculty club, but there was a faculty dining group that avoided dietary (and other) difficulties by admitting no Jews at all.

A non-*Judenrein* faculty club opened a few years after I arrived. The Jewish presence on the Penn faculty, already quite visible in economics, political science, mathematics, and the natural sciences, along with the Wharton School of Business and the law and medical schools, was rising rapidly in more resistant realms such as History and English.

One of my fellow newcomers, sociologist Philip Rieff, corralled me for lunch one day in the new club to recruit for some faculty cause, now mercifully forgotten. "We must form a cadre!" he proclaimed in his best Old Left manner. But our sedate academic watering hole could hardly be compared to, say, a café at the Finland Station (assuming there was one). The faculty club—indeed, the campus—as revolutionary breeding ground was yet to come.

Penn, for all its academic strengths, did not turn out to be quite what I had hoped for. It was still in many respects a pokey sort of place. True, it had many of the attributes of an elite school: age, prominent alums and faculty members, inclusion in the eight-member Ivy League. But it also was at or near the bottom of the Ivy heap in distinction and money, its prowess in football and other sports revealingly suspect. It had a campus with little to be said for it and more Jewish undergraduates than was thought good for it in the eyes of the Philadelphia elite.

Penn, like all universities, was changing rapidly by the late 1950s. But the History Department still was dominated by an older group, with a few distinguished people (diplomatic historian Arthur P. Whitaker, Roy Nichols and Tom Cochran in American political and economic history, Kenneth Setton in medieval history) and a larger set of somewhat dimmer bulbs.

Cochran was one of the more original historians of his time: a pioneer in business history and the application of social science to a discipline that found it hard to break loose from its storytelling base. He was a generous friend and mentor, a charmer who reveled in owning a brace of Mercedes-Benzes and playing ardent golf at a Main Line country club, all the while insisting that he was a Socialist.

Penn in my time gave off increasing signs that it was positioned to benefit from the academic takeoff of the late twentieth century. Each year it responded more to the heady winds of new (often Jewish) people, to new (often federal) money, and to new buildings: one, the Richards Medical Center, by local architectural genius Louis Kahn. But it was also still much in thrall to old ways of doing (or, more likely, not doing) things.

An instance of this transitional phase was my being asked early on by Arthur Whitaker to act as rapporteur to the monthly meetings of the Philadelphia Foreign Policy Association, a self-important group dominated by Old Family Philadelphians who derived much satisfaction from sitting around the table and listening to semi-luminaries from the State Department and other agencies discourse on the woes of the world. I recall being attracted not so much by the extra income (a cool $50 per session) that my attendance and minutes produced, as by the prospect of getting a glimpse of the Philadelphia Club, the towering height of the city's not-inconsequential social pecking order, where the group's dinner meetings were held. Otherwise the Club was closed to Jews: Brotherly Love went only so far.

When I arrived at Penn my yearly teaching load, a not inapt term, was a bracing seven two-hour courses a year, recently cut back from eight. Since I had been teaching eight courses a year in Chapel Hill (though only in two subjects), I mistakenly regarded this as a lesser obligation. I soon discovered that I would have to range far afield from the American history survey and the American political history offerings that were my heart's desire.

This had one potentially beneficial effect. Drawing on my Harvard course-taking with Oscar Handlin, the country's leading immigration historian, I came up with a course on the history of American ethnic groups: a subject then relatively path-breaking and gravid with future potential as a popular realm of teaching and scholarship, which I was not astute enough to capitalize on. Instead, I focused on what became my lifelong scholarly field of interest: American political and economic institutions, and their political, legal, and regulatory milieus.

It is not hard to make a case for the importance and validity of this area of American history, and I would be delighted to do so if anyone asked. But given what was about to explode in the historical profession during the 1960s and 1970s—an all-consuming interest in the themes of race, gender, and class; a steep decline in interest (and for that matter belief) in institutions and their history—it would have been hard to come up with a less propitious career choice. But then, as I suppose my entering the Navy coterminous with the cessation of the Korean War revealed, making dicey career choices was one thing I was good at.

When I came to Penn I was already deep into a new topic: the large life insurance companies in the late nineteenth and early twentieth centuries. How had I come to this? As I remember, chiefly because James M. Beck, my thesis subject, in the course of his career served as counsel for the Mutual Life Insurance Company and while there strongly advocated the federal regulation of life insurance.

Since the greater part of Beck's political career had been devoted to resisting federal intervention in any size, shape, or form, this was . . . interesting. I soon discovered that here, as in so much else, he was responding to his (corporate) master's voice. The Mutual and other large insurance companies were strong advocates of federal regulation of their business not out of a sudden statist epiphany, but because they found in it a handy way of responding to (that is, escaping from) a system of regulation by the states both extensive in structure and costly to circumvent. As Richard McCurdy, the Mutual's president, told his board when presenting a bought-and-paid-for report on the company by a group of state insurance commissioners: "You can take it for what it is worth, although I doubt if you would take it for what it cost." (McCurdy was a refreshing example of the un-circumspect turn-of-the-century corporate chieftain. He once appealed to the Mutual's board against revealing too much of the company's doings to state regulators: "Civilized men cannot perform all the offices of nature upon the sidewalk . . . So the inner workings of the machinery of any technical business cannot be exposed to the observation of the public with propriety.")

In the late 1950s it was still the common belief in the historical literature that corporations in the Gilded Age and the Progressive Era opposed federal authority in all its forms. Some railroads self-interestedly supported the Interstate Commerce Act of 1887, but this was just beginning to be recognized.

The disparity between actual and expected behavior set my historian's antennae quivering. I soon turned to the ten volumes of testimony and exhibits that Charles Evans Hughes extracted from the big insurance companies during the New York Armstrong investigation of 1905. That inquiry was a pioneering evisceration of corporate misdeeds, full of eyebrow-raising revelations. More, it revealed a group of companies whose business careers deviated from the prevailing norm of their counterparts in oil, beef, and the like. So I drifted into an attempt to examine the managerial, business, legal, and political behavior of a group of large industrial and straight life insurance companies: the Prudential and Metropolitan Life, the Mutual, New York Life, and the Equitable.

A digression into the satisfaction potential of historical research, despite its often minimal social and personal returns: I hoped for good pickings in the archives of the Mutual, which my former subject James M. Beck had represented in legal matters. Instead I was put in the hands of a public relations man who plied me with printed handouts extolling the company's virtues. One day, Mutual board chairman Lewis Douglas, a flamboyant business buccaneer who had been a protégé of Beck, swept into the PR office in which I was desultorily turning over the canned pap fed to me. "Where's the fellow who wrote the book on Beck?" he demanded to know. I was duly introduced, Douglas dilated on how important Beck had been to his career, commanded: "Give this young man anything he wants to see!" and swept out along with his entourage.

I was duly taken to a vast warehouse on Manhattan's West Side, where the company's policies were kept. I wandered down the endless corridors, with identical rows of storage boxes on either side. But one aisle looked different: there was a break in what was otherwise an endless sea of unreadable documents. This turned out to be the letterpress copies of company president McCurdy's correspondence around the turn of the century. (So hidden was this treasure trove that Columbia economic historian Shepard Clough, who published an authorized history of the company in 1946, was unaware of its existence.)

I sought to approach the large insurance companies as a distinctive corporate culture: "a society of companies." I didn't have the sociological or economic knowledge or sophistication to develop this concept very far. But I did come to an unexpected conclusion: that the more forcefully the companies sought to control their regulatory/political, legal, and domestic and overseas business environments, the more trouble they got into, in terms of both their financial success and their public-political standing. It was only after the 1905 Armstrong investigation in New York and its subsequent regulatory tightening-up, which stripped away much of the companies' grandiose political and international pretensions, that they entered into a golden age of corporate profitability.

Adolf Berle, New Dealer and co-author of the influential *The Modern Corporation and Private Property*, liked what I had to say about the limits of corporate power. William Appleman Williams, a pioneer in the New Left critique of American imperialism, liked what I had to say about the companies' ambitious overseas ventures. Presumably what both liked most of all was what they saw in the book as confirming their own predilections. That, alas, appears to be a major function of the discipline of history.

For all its stylistic awkwardness and lack of theoretical sophistication, the book struck a chord sufficiently strong for Handlin to induce his colleagues to have me invited to come to Harvard

in 1960–1961 as a visiting lecturer. (Having just become an associate professor at Penn, I was not quite in the visiting professor
category. One member of the department, I was told, said of my
appointment, "My, he's come a long way." In the same welcoming spirit, the student course guide reported to its readers that it
knew nothing of me or my university.)

I was to teach the year-long course in American Political History customarily given by the leave-taking Frank Freidel. I tried
to approach the subject much as Handlin had done with American social history and as my Penn mentor Tom Cochran had
done with his influential assault on the "presidential synthesis"
that defined American political history by its chief executives. I
tried to look at large themes stretching over considerable periods
of time rather than chop things up into bite-sized "ages" (of
Jackson, of Roosevelt) or "eras" (of Good Feelings, of Progressivism). How American historians love to speak of ages and eras
that are ten or fifteen years long! I imagine it is a form of compensation for the relative brevity of our history, compared to
Old Europe and Old Asia.

The easy digestibility of political history and its enhanced
appeal to Harvard undergraduates, many of whom in the age of
President John F. Kennedy nourished expectations of running
the country themselves some day (later that outreach would
extend to the world), assured me a large and receptive student
audience. And Vietnam had not yet moved my decidedly un-
radical take on the American past beyond the pale of acceptable
discourse.

I became even trendier when, in November, Kennedy was
murdered. In those innocent days, history still was regarded as
a subject with something to teach the present, and I was fre-
quently called on to explain the incomprehensible. I did a spate

of *Boston Globe* reviews of books on Lee Harvey Oswald and the assassination.

My take on the tragedy was that it was yet another instance of a sadly recurring record of deranged loners setting out to kill our presidents: successfully in the cases of Abraham Lincoln, James Garfield, William McKinley, and Kennedy; unsuccessfully in the cases of Andrew Jackson, FDR (when he was still president-elect), Harry Truman, Gerald Ford, and Ronald Reagan. I observed that each of the successful attempts was by a perpetrator whose psychosis fed on larger discontents. Thus John Wilkes Booth battened on the fall of the Confederacy; Garfield's assassin, Charles Guiteau, saw himself as a disappointed office-seeker, reflecting the boss-and-patronage-ridden party politics of the time; McKinley's assassin, Leon Czolgosz, identified with the fevered grievances of turn-of-the-century anarchists.

And Lee Harvey Oswald? His context was the anti-American side of the cold war: a claim to Marxism, a short-lived defection to the Soviet Union, participation in the pro-Castro Fair Play for Cuba Committee, a (literal) shot at right-wing General Edwin Walker.

This was hardly what left-liberal academics and literary intellectuals hungered to hear. The spread of postwar prosperity and the revelation of Soviet dictator Joseph Stalin's crimes made the old Marxist Left marginal compared to its salad days in the Great Depression and the war against fascism. But Third World causes—the fight against colonialism in Asia, Africa, and the Middle East; the fight against white racism and black segregation in the United States—were beginning to make the Left more appealing. New heroes—Fidel Castro, Mao Tse-tung— eased the path of avoiding the embarrassing subject of the crimes of Uncle Joe.

On the cusp of the Left's revival under the spurs of Vietnam and civil rights, it was necessary that JFK's assassination be stripped of any Castroite or other Left-Communist imputations. In any case, the Left's ideological mindset, in which chance and individual choice had little purchase, was disinclined to accept a lone-nut theory. Yet it was difficult to convincingly locate Oswald in the cesspools of the Right.

Instead, in a bizarre replay of the Stalinist conspiracy fantasies of the 1930s Purge Trials and the McCarthyite Communist-conspiratorialism of the 1950s, the Left began to spin a tale of plotting at the highest levels of government. It was kicked off, appropriately, not by some hardened apparatchik but by a representative figure from the new breeding-ground of the Left: burgeoning academe. Richard Popkin, a philosophy professor at the University of California at San Diego, knew about as much about the assassination of Kennedy as Harvard English professor Elaine Scarry did about the crash of TWA Flight 800 in 1996, when she ascribed it to the non-accidental launch of Navy missiles. Both the Popkin and the Scarry revelations appeared in the *New York Review of Books*, the organ of the Left-literary-academic audience which would be most ready to swallow these fabulist Jonahs whole.

As my Harvard year progressed, I was approached by Brandeis, a small new university down the Charles River in Waltham. If Harvard undergrads knew little about Penn, I knew even less about Brandeis. Nor was there, in truth, much to know. It had gone into business in 1948, the same year as the creation of Israel, the product of not dissimilar social and cultural forces.

In the wake of the Second World War, the idea took hold among American Jews that they had a heightened obligation to create a secular, nonsectarian university, as their Protestant fellow-citizens had done in centuries past. One group, centered in New York, envisioned a campus in Westchester County named after Albert Einstein and headed by the English socialist and political theorist Harold Laski. Here was intellectual horse-power on a large scale. But there was no one to gather the resources necessary for so costly a start-up as a college. And it is hard in retrospect to imagine so mercurial a personality as Laski tending to the mundane demands of university-making.

Instead, a confluence of happenstances gave Brandeis an auspicious start in life. A group of primarily Boston-based Jewish businessmen, most of them with no competing college commitment and spurred perhaps by the double-whammy anti-Semitism emanating from both Brahmin and Irish Boston, were drawn to the idea of a Jewish-sponsored school.

Then the eccentrically philo-Semitic John Hall Smith, who founded and presided over Middlesex Medical College, an unaccredited medical school in the Boston suburb of Waltham that in practice turned out veterinarians, offered his campus and charter to the Brandeis founders as a gift. He had only two stipulations: that there be no racial, religious, or gender restrictions; and that his son, C. Ruggles Smith, have a lifetime job at the university. (And so he did, as its first general counsel.)

The third, and determining, piece of the Brandeis-creation puzzle was the appearance of Abram L. Sachar as its first president. He was in the classic mold of brilliant entrepreneurs. That it was education rather than oil, steel, or railroads to which he applied his talents mattered little. He had the insight to see the fund-raising potential of the message that a Jewish-sponsored nonsectarian college marked the emergence of Jews as full-fledged members of the American community: "A Host at Last," as his splendidly self-serving history of the university put it.

By the time I came there, Brandeis was seventeen years old, a feisty adolescent of a school. It had an unusually large number of gifted students, the product of lingering anti-Semitism in the admissions offices of the elite colleges and the appeal of a place whose faculty had more than its share of celebrities. Among these were literary critics Irving Howe and Philip Rahv, public intellectual Max Lerner, historian Frank Manuel, sociologist Lewis Coser, psychologist Abraham Maslow, and soon-to-be-world-famous radical theorist Herbert Marcuse.

It is hard, even now, for me to judge the degree to which I was attracted to Brandeis by its Jewishness. Certainly I had no religious tie; and much of my career to date had been spent in institutions—the Navy, North Carolina, Penn—not notable for a significant Jewish presence. And our social life was defined more by the character of postwar America at large than by a Jewish religious identity.

But in retrospect I can see that a combination of factors was in fact drawing us ineluctably into a Jewish-Americanness that made Brandeis a readily acceptable choice. One of these was family, my wife Phyllis's more than mine. (She *had* a family, in the traditional sense of sisters, brothers, cousins, aunts and uncles; beyond my parents, I did not.) Another was our going from the Navy to the academic culture in the late 1950s. We had Jewish friends in Chapel Hill and more at Penn, which I suppose did involve some social cherry-picking. This may have been in part a defensive measure when Jews still had something of an outlander status. As time passed, and the number of Jews in academia grew geometrically, to be part of a Jewish faculty scene became a norm, not an abnorm.

Like so many of my generation, I was attracted by Jewish culture, from food and humor to politics and intellectual life. (Black culture would have a similar appeal to the baby boomers of the 1960s and 1970s; there are signs that Islamic culture has a similar appeal in advanced social circles today.) When I came out to have lunch with my Brandeis recruiters, historian Leonard Levy and political scientist John Roche, the *plat du jour* at the Faculty Club was a memorable compound of London broil with béarnaise sauce and potato kugel: a perfect expression of the school's dual pretentions to the academic scene at large and to its Jewish Ur-identity.

Even more tempting was the proposal to start up a PhD program in the History of American Civilization. How could a small new school such as Brandeis have the chutzpah (it is hard to think of a more applicable use of the word) to be rushing headlong into PhD-granting status? Because of a weird turn of the legal-regulatory wheel: the kind of serendipity that I would spend much of my history-writing career fastening upon, and savoring.

John Hall Smith, the proprietor of Middlesex Medical College, originally named his institution the University of Massachusetts. He had the grandiosely eccentric idea of giving his med-vet students a smattering and more of the humanities. (The school's main building was a low-budget attempt to recreate a medieval castle.) Smith appointed Joseph Cheskis, a polymath Lithuanian Jewish immigrant, to be his school's professor of humanities. (Brandeis inherited Cheskis as its first teacher of Romance languages. The earliest generations of Brandeis graduates, so it was said, emerged speaking French and Spanish—insofar as they did so—with a rich Lithuanian Yiddish accent.)

Smith was approached by the Commonwealth in the 1930s to give up his school's title of the University of Massachusetts. The state was upgrading its cow college, and wanted the name. Smith agreed on condition that his school's charter be amended to allow his now-renamed Middlesex Medical College to have MA- and PhD-granting powers. That right was passed on to Brandeis. And so the new school was able to stick its toe in graduate-degree waters without having to run a gauntlet of opposition from the existing barons in the state's Ed Biz.

What proved to be decisive in our decision to move from Penn to Brandeis was the appeal of Cambridge and the non-appeal of Philadelphia. Our Cambridge year, which was spent in a rented house a short walk from the Harvard campus, was a revelation to a family whose living experience until then fit the postwar middle-class American suburban ideal. Our son, now about eleven years old, suddenly found himself in a welter of institutionalized instruction: basketball at the Cambridge Y, clarinet-playing at the Longy School of Music. One day he asked his mother, "Are we Jewish?" She assured him that indeed we were, except that we didn't go to synagogue; we weren't practicing Jews. "Thank God!" was his response. "If I had to practice one more thing I'd go out of my mind."

While I was indisputably a member of Brandeis's Department of History, and indeed served an extended sentence as chairman, my strongest institutional affiliation was with our doctoral program in the History of American Civilization. In part this was because Brandeis's pioneering graduate programs— biochemistry, history of ideas—tended to cut across the usual departmental lines. Why so? Because traditional disciplines in this fledgling school were thin in numbers and spotty in quality. And in each department the strongest faculty members tended to be iconoclastic types. The anti-Semitic academic past, the strong contrarian strain in Jewish intellectual life, and, I suppose, the very newness of Brandeis attracted oddballs more readily than establishmentarians, which made for a readiness to operate outside traditional disciplinary boundaries.

The core group of Americanists who kicked things off in the History of American Civilization Program were Leonard Levy, John Roche, David Hackett Fischer, Marvin Meyers, and yours truly. A motley crew we were, and so we remained.

Leonard Levy grew up in St. Louis but his academic style so far as I could determine was shaped by his World War II experience. He was attached to an Army Military Police unit charged with the unpalatable task of guarding hard-core Nazi prisoners of war in remote camps in the less-gardenlike parts of states such as Montana and Arkansas. Leonard appears to have spent his war being promoted to sergeant, having one of the prisoners refer slightingly to him as a dirty Jew or the like, chastising the wayward charge by breaking his arm with his rifle butt, and being reduced to private.

These were the background and mindset that Leonard brought to Columbia, where at war's end he entered graduate school, aiming to become (who knows how or why) an American constitutional historian. So did his fellow student Harold Hyman, who like Levy became a distinguished scholar in that field. Hyman supposedly spent time in a high school for incorrigible youths, was a Marine sergeant in the first wave at Guadalcanal, and, while more soft-spoken than Levy, was not one whit less a force of nature. Their dazed fellow students soon dubbed them the Tiger and the Shark.

Leonard was dean of faculty when I came to Brandeis, tough and smart enough to deal with the self-absorbed public intellectuals and perks-obsessed mediocrities on the faculty, as well as with Abram Sachar, a great institution-builder fully endowed with the monomaniacal self-confidence that goes with that talent. After we moved up from Philadelphia, I gave Leonard my moving bill. (Brandeis in those early days was nothing if not hands-on.) He looked at it and truculently asked if I had it in writing that Brandeis would pay the tab. When I assured him that I did, he reluctantly agreed to pay up. I came home that night and my wife asked me what it was like there. I told her that it was too early to bring on the women and children.

His smarts and toughness shaped Leonard's scholarly work as well. His iconoclastic book *Jefferson and Civil Liberties: The Darker Side* (1963) popularized a side of Jefferson that had slid into obscurity during the New Deal-and-after years. *The Origins of the Fifth Amendment* (1968) definitively traced the sources of a cornerstone of the American civil liberties tradition and won him a Pulitzer in History.

Levy's closest colleague was politics professor John P. Roche, as feisty secular Irish as Levy was feisty secular Jewish. John put in grunt service both as a token non-Jewish Trotskyite on the eve of World War II and as a soldier during the war. His most influential scholarly work was an *American Political Science Review* article that examined the Constitutional Convention of 1787 as an exceptionally skilled political caucus. This was a shrewd counter to the deification of the Founders as larger than life, the traditional take on the subject, or their denigration as a bunch of self-interested oligarchs, popular on the Left since Charles A. Beard's 1912 book made that argument. It was a refreshingly realistic, down-to-earth piece of work. In this sense it was very much part of the more cold-eyed, but at the same time more appreciative, approach to the American past that came into favor in the wake of the Depression's end and Nazism's defeat.

The third leg in the American civilization group was Marvin Meyers, whose classic work *The Jacksonian Persuasion* (1957) did for Andrew Jackson and his followers what Levy was doing to and for the history of civil liberties and Roche for the Founding Fathers: at one and the same time demystifying their subjects and adding to the weight of their place in American history.

The youngest member of our Gang of Five was David Hackett Fischer, whose WASP.y background (his father headed Baltimore's school system, and David had been an F. Scott Fitzgerald-like hell-raising undergraduate at Princeton) was bizarrely at odds with Brandeis's dominant middle-class Jewish culture.

But apparently this well suited David's highly developed iconoclastic streak. In 1965 he published *Historians' Fallacies*, an evisceration of the all-too-common inadequacies that peppered the writings of his fellow American historians. When a reviewer took him to task for giving his Brandeis colleagues a pass, he indignantly responded that he was at least as unsparing of their deficiencies as of anyone else's.

Nor did he exempt himself from the need to cleanse his own stable. His colleague Leonard Levy was asked to review a new (and highly original) book by David on the Federalists. Leonard thought this an improper request and told David about it. Characteristically, he asked if he could write the review under Leonard's name; Leonard, characteristically, agreed. But when he saw David's self-review, he refused to submit it: it was far too critical.

A year or two after I came to Brandeis, our American history group got a financial fillip that made our graduate program a more-than-going concern. Abe Sachar used his fundraising talents to induce Irving Crown, of a wealthy Chicago family, to make a then-handsome commitment to a $75,000-a-year donation, primarily for student fellowships, to stretch for twenty years. This enabled us to compete with the nation's top graduate programs in American history. And our group had the academic credentials (burnished in later years by the addition of Stephan Thernstrom, John Demos, and James Kloppenberg) to induce good students to come.

This in turn made for a strong collective sense among both faculty and students that ours was a graduate program with a special élan. The resulting enthusiasm became a powerful recruiting tool for new students, and made for a notably successful doctoral program. A national poll of American history graduate students some years ago concluded that it was the country's best.

So I was part of a pretty high-powered group. While I had been productive for a historian of my age, I couldn't be said to have significantly shaped the course of historical research. Still, I had had some impact. About the time I went to Brandeis, I was asked to write the late nineteenth century volume in a projected Oxford History of the United States, whose editors were Richard Hofstadter and C. Vann Woodward: as good as it gets. Flushed with pride, I showed the letter, which listed the other participants, to my wife, Phyllis. She quickly put me in my place: "My, this *is* a distinguished list. You're the only one I've never heard of."

Manfully I overcame this affectionately ironic compliment. I interpreted my charge as an examination primarily of American politics, law, and government. Here was the germ of future trouble. I must have assumed that it was OK from my dealings with editor Hofstadter. But he died in 1970 and my contacts with Woodward, who had a more inclusive view of things, were infrequent. So misunderstanding grew like mushrooms in a dark cellar.

Faced with limitless sources, both manuscript and printed, I settled on the strategy of focusing on contemporary books, pamphlets, and magazine articles. I made my selections by going through major finding aids of those pre-computer days: the Harvard Library's printed catalogues of books by call numbers, arranged in chronological order; and for articles, *Poole's Index, The Reader's Guide to Periodical Literature,* and *The Index to Legal Periodicals.* I made a few forays into what I thought might be promising manuscript collections in places such as the Library of Congress and the Wisconsin Historical Society Library. But the fragmentary nature of these excursions made them frosting on a cake whose substance was composed of the printed outpouring of what was, after all, a great age of American periodicals.

As in my previous book on life insurance, I set out to describe how a major American institution—or in this case, three of them: politics, government, and law—responded to the challenges of their time. Before, I had examined the workings of what I called a society of companies. Now, I adopted the organizing concept of an American *polity*: an interrelated web of political (parties, elections, office-holding, legislation), governmental (bureaucracy and the State, political theory), and legal (lawyers, courts, the law) institutions.

I called the book *Affairs of State: Public Life in Late Nineteenth-Century America*: descriptive enough. (Historian Jean Baker wrote a book called *Affairs of Party* some years later. I mentioned the similarity to her, and she said that of course she stole it. In fact it was no theft, any more than my book was the first to use the title—only the kind of useful appropriation that scholarship is supposed to be about.)

My approach helped me with the problem of describing how American politics, government, and law worked in the years dominated by the Civil War and large-scale industrialization. I carved this lump of history into two big chunks, which I labeled The Postwar Polity (how our public institutions responded to the experience, and then the aftermath, of the Civil War and the end of slavery) and The Industrial Polity (how politics, government, and law shifted from a fixation on the issues of union, slavery, and race to the issues of industrial, agricultural, urban, and immigration takeoff).

No one had tried to blend political, legal, and governmental history on this scale before. I thought I had taken a pretty big bite out of the American history pie, including lots of new stuff on how the pols, the judges, the legislatures, and the bureaucrats, national and state, wrestled with the most compelling economic and social issues of the time: regulation, interest groups, economic growth, race, crime, family life, and the like. And I had an untypical perspective. I held that in the course of American history, *continuity* was at least as conspicuous as the *change* that historians so preferred to talk about. This continuity was not so much of policy but of tensions over policy: between individualism and social order, localism and centralism, laissez-faire and the active state, inclusive and restrictive views of American citizenship.

Editor Woodward not unreasonably wanted the Oxford History volumes to deal more directly with the economic (and particularly the ever-hotter new social) history of the nation. Having put years of work into what became a six hundred-page book, I wasn't ready to go back to the drawing board. So we parted. I had to get a new publisher and Harvard helpfully stepped in, giving the book a good sendoff as one of its glitzy new Belknap Press imprints.

Affairs of State has had a pretty long life for an American history book, and lots of people in the know have said nice things about it. But it never won anything near blockbuster (more accurately, anything more than light explosive) status in the world of American historical writing. Far be it from me to argue that it was undervalued; the history book market works about as well as any. I do think that the kind of history I was writing was ill-timed in the sense that when it appeared, in 1977, it was unlikely to win friends and influence people through its subject matter or by its relatively non-ideological tone (though of course neither Marxists nor postmodernists would say that such a thing is possible).

I wasn't the only one in my business to feel the effect of rapid cultural change. The academy in general, and Brandeis in particular, suffered from the combined ailments of the 1970s: inflation, a falling stock market and declining revenue, faculty and students in a continuing state of demoralization after the tectonic shifts of the late sixties.

The emoluments of late twentieth-century American academic life had to do constant battle with darker clouds of attitude and behavior ever more evident on the horizon. The student uprisings of the late sixties and early seventies had a more traumatic impact on the academic *arrivistes* of my generation than on the Old Boys who dated from the pre-Jewish, pre-World War II past. The latter were not unfamiliar, as we were, with undergraduates raising hell (although claiming to be doing it for noble causes was something new). And many of the hell-raisers were hardly scholarship boys, but rather came from old WASP families or new upper-professional Jewish ones.

The academics who took the sixties hard were different from their predecessors. Some were escapees from Hitler or Stalin, or both, who detected a whiff of fascism or bolshevism in the protest air. Many more were not unlike myself: of middle- or working-class backgrounds, often Jewish, not religious but in compensation heavily invested emotionally in a view of the university as a place where reason and intellect prevailed and where students gratefully absorbed what their teachers taught. To be a professor was, magically, to be invested with many of the good things in life: ample time to do what you most wanted to do, reasonable compensation, paid-for trips to conferences, and teaching gigs in attractive locales.

Now this utopia was under siege from youths who dressed, looked, and talked like barbarians at the gate. They claimed to be free from—and unalterably opposed to—the values of liberalism, academic freedom, and the university as an ivory tower devoted to the pursuit of truth, on which so many of us had hung our lives, our fortunes, and our sacred (now scared) honor.

Some of us took it harder than others. Perhaps the closest correlation was with the degree and kind of radicalism practiced in our youth. My Brandeis colleagues most affected by the student upsurge often had been Trotskyites, or members of even more obscure left-wing sects, before the war. Now they sought respectability and a peaceful academic life; but once again history was conspiring to betray their hopes. Those like myself who were a bit younger, and a lot less radical and/or politically engaged, took it all with less of a sense of personal betrayal—or, as I suspect the ex-radicals thought, with the same propensity for waffling and opting out that we had shown in other issues of public and intellectual life.

The harmful consequences of the student rebellion were visible across the academic scene. But they were especially severe at Brandeis, one of the more conspicuous locales for the anti-Vietnam and, more particularly, the militant black demonstrations of the time.

In 1968, founder Sachar retired—although "retired" is not quite the right word: he continued to be a looming presence as chancellor, occupying a Mussolini-like office and regarding his successors much as Margaret Thatcher did hers. Appropriately, his offspring was twenty-one years old. A series of post-Sachar presidents proved unable to surmount the problem of identity. Was Brandeis to be a Jewish-sponsored secular-intellectual university? Or, given the easy access of bright Jews to the nation's top schools, should it focus on those applicants religious enough, and not-so-exceptional enough, to be induced to come? Faculty quality declined, as the cream tended either to curdle with age or, if still tasty, to be lured away to the ever-larger body of schools able and willing to outbid Brandeis. I remember one dark day when the four senior members of the American history program shared outside approaches currently under consideration: Keller and MIT, Meyers and Maryland, Fischer and the University of Washington, Demos and the University of Wisconsin.

This coincided with (and was closely related to) a steep decline in the university's finances and the quality of its student intake. The blend of Brandeis's particular problems and the more general malaise affecting American higher education made the 1970s and 1980s a toxic time, from which neither Brandeis nor its inhabitants ever fully recovered.

But in other respects my academic life if anything got better: there still was a wave to be ridden. *Affairs of State* led to an invitation to visit Oxford in 1981–1982 as the Harmsworth Professor of American History (or, as I came to see it, giving Oxford its Harmsworth). [Plate 13] Every American, especially an Academic-American, has to work through a complicated relationship with that most Freudian of all places, the Mother Country. For many, ranging from those born to the Anglo-Saxon persuasion to assimilationist Jews of the S.J. Perelman persuasion, the English part-fantasy of high intelligence, great manners, well-cut clothes, and tons of history (all clad in a language so familiar that it takes the travail out of travel) produces an Anglophilia nicely caught by writer Finley Peter Dunne's comic character Mr. Dooley commenting on Woodrow Wilson's ambassador to the Court of St. James: "When the King summoned him to an audience, he came as fast as his hands and knees could carry him."

I confess to sharing some portion of that social attitude. I was a visiting professor at the University of Sussex in 1968 when that school was at the height of its trendiness. And I gave the Commonwealth Lecture at University College London in 1979, in tinglingly close proximity to the mummified Jeremy Bentham.

But I never deluded myself into thinking that I was anything more than an *en passant* sojourner to Albion's shores. So while I duly paid homage to the age and beauty of Oxford's colleges, the wit and polish of the London stage, and the loveliness of chunks of the English countryside, a part of me could not help but approach my Harmsworth year in the persona of an anthropologist on an extended field trip, observing the ways of an at-times bizarre tribe.

I was substantially helped in this mindset by the character of Queen's, the College bestowed with—or burdened by—the care and feeding of the visiting Harmsworth professor. Unlike a widening swath of Oxford (and indeed British) life, Queen's at that time still was resolutely committed to the Old Ways: a world view whose roots, still visible, reached back to its founding in 1341.

A few high points, offered in the hope that they don't fall completely into the category of the self-centered traveler ruthlessly imposing his slides on a captive audience:

- At my first Fellow's meeting at Queen's, I was privy to the following sequence of agenda items: a few minutes' desultory discussion, followed by unanimous agreement on the year's College budget of several million pounds; and then a spirited forty-five minute debate, with strong feelings manifested on both sides, over who was responsible for the ivy on the College walls: the Committee on the Garden or the Committee on the Fabric.

- It was at Queen's that I caught a glimpse of what, if the professoriat had its way, would be the academic future. After two thirds of a millennium in the business, Oxford professors (as opposed to the heavily worked tutors) had teaching responsibilities that, if foreshortened further, ran the risk of their losing the power of speech.

- The Ozlike quality of the Gothic surroundings, omnipresent gowns, quite good food and wine at the daily meals, and more-than-quite-good victuals at the not-infrequent gaudies (banquets) was ratcheted up another notch when, in the spring of 1982, the Queen Mother, the Patroness of the College, paid her quinquennial visit. The College was buffed and polished within an inch of its 650-year-old life. The Queen Mum helicoptered into town and met crisply with the faculty assembled in the College's Elizabethan library. (She got out of there as soon as she could, and spent much of the rest of her visit with the College Football team.) Introduced to the visiting American professor, she asked me to which university I belonged. "Brandeis, ma'am," I replied. She sighed a little sigh, and acutely observed: "There are so many new universities today." Thus began and ended my dealings with royalty.

But this was better than the experience of Harvard Dean of Faculty Jeremy Knowles when he was presented to the queen to be invested with an OBE. As he approached, a flunky whispered into the queen's ear that Knowles was from Harvard. But there was a failure to communicate. She warmly greeted him as he approached: "Ah, Cardiff."

CHAPTER FIVE

Family Matters

U ntil now I have glossed over the central feature of my life: not my career, which went well enough, but my private life, which went even better. It is not exactly mainstream nowadays to limit oneself to one marriage, now getting on to sixty years, and two children whose disappointment-and-grief output has been as vanishingly small as their success-and-gratification output has been satisfactorily large.

Let's start with my wife, Phyllis. In 1946, when we met (or, more accurately, were programmed to meet), we lived precisely one block apart in Forest Hills. This was equivalent to two families from the same village in the Pale coming to America on immigrant ships and settling in adjoining Lower East Side tenements.

The ties that bound us inexorably multiplied. We went to the same primary and high schools; we were overlapping members of our high school newspaper's editorial board (though we didn't know each other, as befitted a large public institution). We had intellectual presumptions that set us apart from most of our peers, though Phyllis was far more popular, and academically precocious, than I.

Encrusted in legend, though preserving a residue of truth, is the received family version of how we came (or were brought) together. Our mothers, so the tale goes, met one day at the meat counter at Bohack's, the local market, and commiserated with each other over a pair of children whose proclivity for reading might well put their marriageability at risk. (Phyllis strenuously denies the second half of this narrative, arguing with much credibility that she faced no such threat.) In any event, the two mothers cooked up the idea of a date, and through devices which I have long and mercifully suppressed, I was induced to go along. Off we went to a bracing three hours-plus of *Les Enfants du Paradis*. Our cultural bona fides thus secured, things went swimmingly from there.

What does this say about courting customs in our middle-class enclave? The substantial grounds for compatibility, and the proactivity of our mothers, speak volumes. So does the (in retrospect) inexorable sequence from first-encounter movie-going to a wedding five years later, after we finished our college BAs (Phyllis at Barnard, I at Rochester) and MAs (Phyllis at Columbia, I at Harvard). Both of us, in short, were very much part of the national postwar saga of upward educational mobility. And our tale reinforces the *aperçu* of a contemporary that in our generation, you got married in order to meet girls.

There was notably little parental resistance to our intent to marry in the fall of 1951 before I began my second year at Harvard. (In our station of life, pegging things to the rhythm of the academic year was as natural as acting in tune with the harvest would have been in the peasant societies tucked back in our immigrant ancestry.) To some degree, this stemmed from a shared relief that the mothers' initiative had paid off so hand-somely. And in part, we mischievously liked to think, it might have reflected the belief on each side that the other family was richer.

The wedding itself was not without its strains. Phyllis's father gave us the choice of a full-scale event with all the social trim-mings or a scaled down immediate-family-only ceremony in the rabbi's study, followed by lunch—the saved wedding costs to accrue to us. But financial prudence had a minor role in Phyllis's insistence on a mini-wedding. She had nightmares for years over her older sister's wedding, where she was subjected to the physi-cal imposition of being required to remove her glasses before sashaying (or in her case groping) down the aisle as the maid of honor.

With only a handful of our nearest and dearest bearing wit-ness, we were joined in the study of the rabbi of New York's chi-chi Temple Emanu-El and then adjourned to a luncheon at the dining room of the Hotel Pierre down the street for what my mother, in an untypical flash of anger, called "a businessman's lunch."

Only afterward did we realize how much this must have hurt my mother. The no-holds-barred nuptials of her older sister four or five years before had suppressed any taste on Phyllis's part for further social display. But my mother had not had a crack at a full-fledged wedding, and now there would be no further oppor-tunity to do so.

Before the wedding baked meats were cold, we were on our way to a brief honeymoon in the Adirondacks and then settled into a cozy one-room basement abode ("apartment" would be a pretentious description) in Cambridge. Phyllis's mother eased our journey to the Antipodes by providing us with cans of Del

Monte sliced peaches, clearly not available in so remote a back-water as the one we were headed to.

Since the age of sentience Phyllis had shown a strong aversion to the pink side of her gender. Dolls had no place in her child-hood; tomboying it with the lads was her style. She initially had a desire to be that then most unladylike of things, a doctor. But her aversion to viewing a surgical procedure (admittedly a draw-back) and family pressure to take up a more accessible and lady-like career such as school teaching led her to conclude that by studying literature she could combine her taste for reading with her intellectual ambitions.

But while I got on with my PhD, all the while sustaining a spirited dialogue with my draft board, Phyllis soon demonstrated that under her Lit Crit gloss was exceptional administrative abil-ity. Her educational credentials included a Barnard BA in English literature and a Columbia MA in American literature, capped by a crash course in shorthand and typing at Miss Delehanty's Secretarial School.

This greased the way to a $50-a-week secretarial job working for the associate dean of Harvard's Graduate School of Educa-tion. Phyllis was blessed with a boss who had both a passion for golf and the wit to see that his new secretary could easily do much of what he was supposed to do, and then some. In no time she was in effect running the office. It is hard in retrospect to say what is most revealing about this episode: the vast untapped store of talent among the (still) skirted players in the game of postwar American life, or the vast underutilization of those skills.

My Navy peregrinations and two children put a stop to her proto-career after I left Harvard in 1953. Phyllis devoted herself to the care and upbringing of an infant daughter in the inauspicious ambience of Adak in the Aleutians, and then of two small children in the more benign world of garden apartment-suburbia in Falls Church and Chapel Hill.

When we moved to Philadelphia, things changed. The children went to The School in Rose Valley, an idyllic, Quaker-spirited country day school near us. (Something of its culture may be gleaned from an incident that occurred when we were driving with our children from Philadelphia to New York. To keep them from eating each other, we proposed a word game. When asked who would go first, two chubby hands went up and two piping voices called out in unison: "Second!")

Despite our outlander status, in no time Phyllis was a parent member of the School's board. And as soon as the children were irrevocably enmeshed in the education maze, she enrolled in Penn's PhD program in American Civilization. Two major spurs: her father agreed to pony up the tuition (not necessary after her first year; thereafter the university footed the bill); and a friend pointed out the substantially higher financial rewards that came from an academic career graced by a PhD.

This is not to say that matters of the mind were absent on leave. Phyllis, like me, was increasingly aware that we lived in a time of special change, and promise, in American life. The Great Depression and World War II were sliding into the dimly remembered past; prosperity and promise unrolled like a magic carpet before us. (Though when I asked a seminar at my home of otherwise fashionably skeptical-about-America Penn seniors how many expected to live better than their parents did, all raised their hands. Then I asked how many did not expect to live as well as their parents. One hand went up: Phyllis's.)

Appealing to her, too, may have been the social-sciencey character of Penn's American Civilization program. It was sort of hit-and-miss: a dab of cultural anthropology here, a smidgeon of archeology-colored study of artifacts there. (For a while, Phyllis developed an exotic interest in the porringers turned out by Philadelphia's Huguenots.)

We moved to Cambridge in 1963, while she was midstream in the Penn program. She went back for her oral exam, awash with uncertainty over whether her program of self-study would fill the bill. (It was reported to me, perhaps exaggeratedly, that she had to be quickly awarded "distinction" and be removed from the examination room, all the while giving more fulsome and informed answers to her questions than anyone expected, or indeed imagined was possible.)

In this, the dawning of the Age of the Lib, Phyllis got on with finishing her dissertation and starting her career within the confines imposed by motherhood and wifehood. She managed the first by drawing not so much on (lackadaisical) supervision from Penn, as on the Cambridge academic community in which we lived, and on her own indomitable will. In (by PhD standards) short order she wrote an innovative and imaginatively conceived thesis on the impact of America's entry into World War I on three German-American intellectuals. These were Hermann Hagedorn, a poet and Theodore Roosevelt biographer, who became a great advocate of the Allies and then of America's war effort; man of letters George Sylvester Viereck, who became a German spy; and Harvard psychology professor Hugo Münsterberg, who tried to intermediate between his German past and his American present, and for his pains suffered a fatal heart attack in 1916.

In each case, Phyllis unearthed diaries and letters dating from her subjects' youth and blended their intellectual and political journeys with their psychological predispositions. Harvard published the finished product in 1979 as *States of Belonging: German-American Intellectuals and the First World War.*

Penn gave her a PhD with distinction in 1969, just in time for the beginning of the post-civil rights, post-Vietnam feminist onslaught on the country's tottery male citadels. Compared to those other bones of national contention, the Lib was a mild-mannered upheaval: a velvet revolution. For Phyllis, as for many in her situation, the first break was not a full-scale academic appointment, still widely regarded as the prerogative of real (and even not so real) men, but a fellowship at the Bunting (later renamed the Radcliffe) Institute, established to provide a place to work for female academics, artists, and writers. She spent two years turning her dissertation into a book, a process not unlike alchemy in that it sought to turn a baser metal into gold.

Never one to toot her own horn, Phyllis had to endure one evening at a friend's house dominated by the fulminations of a novelist whose self-esteem substantially outweighed her literary gifts. She told her captive audience that her litany of achievements included nearly getting a fellowship at the Bunting Institute. Soon after, Phyllis swam into her ken, and she graciously asked: "And what do you do, my dear? Are you a happy little housewife?" "No," said Phyllis, unable to let such an opportunity glide by, "I'm a fellow at the Bunting Institute."

After two years of being alienated by the more bizarre forms of feminism blossoming in the Institute hothouse, Phyllis entered the college market—if so resolutely anti-commercial a world as academia can be so characterized. Teaching leads still were scarce outside of women's colleges; male faculty were not yet acclimatized to the New World A-Comin'. One Harvard professor called Phyllis to task for seeking an academic job, and thus depriving some worthy young man of his God-given right to preference over women. Another graciously told her that while he had had a number of female graduate students, none, to his regret, had mastered the architectonics of a dissertation.

Then Holy Cross College in Worcester asked her to come as director of special studies—in effect, to oversee the honors program and other not strictly departmental activities. This was hardly cutting-edge stuff, or up to her qualifications. But her predecessor had come to the job from loftier origins. Dorothy Marshall had been dean of Bryn Mawr since 1947. In 1970 she moved with her husband, who had a new job in Massachusetts, and took what she could get: the newly created special studies post at Holy Cross.

But the earthworks defending the academy against women were crumbling fast. Within a year Marshall went off to be provost at UMass Boston, at that time one of the more conspicuous positions held by a woman in a mixed-gender university.

Much as a decade and more before I had been well-placed to ride the wave stirred by the collapse of academic anti-Semitism, so now was Phyllis propelled by the very similar sea change going on in gender attitudes. Professorial careers were rapidly opening to female academics, and so they did for administrators. Phyllis spent two happy and successful years at Holy Cross. She got on famously with the faculty's Jesuits, less famously with the lay faculty. (Once a group of her faculty friends were jokingly discussing the prospect of a movie being made of a colleague's book on American Catholicism. Phyllis demurely asked if she might not play the part of Mother Church.)

In 1973 economist Henry Rosovsky became dean of the Faculty of Arts and Sciences at Harvard, making him the first Jew to get a prominent administrative place in FAS, that bastion of Old Harvard. He asked Phyllis (whom he knew socially) to succeed the retiring affirmative action officer then on hand. She was ready to take on this task but wanted guarantees that if (as she expected) she could do the job with one hand, the other would be allowed to deal with matters more central to the doings of the faculty.

Now her most notable skills—high intelligence and administrative talent, perfect pitch in speaking and understanding Academese—came into play. The challenge was not a minor one. Soon after she arrived, a senior FAS administrator—Harvard College grad, male—came to instruct this outlandish newcomer in her new life. "You must always remember that you work for Harvard," he sententiously declaimed. "No, _____," she mischievously replied. "I don't work for Harvard; I work for money." (At her retirement dinner she recalled this greeting, but conceded that in fact she did indeed work for Harvard, and co-wrote Harvard's history—adding that Dean Rosovsky saw to it that she didn't work for money.)

Coming to terms with a faculty not noted for its self-abnegation was also necessary. Early on she arrived at a dinner meeting with a conspicuously (though by no means uniquely) self-regarding and socially pretentious professor. He gazed around the room, and observed, "I see that there are place cards at the settings. Your work, no doubt, my dear." "No, Sidney," she replied. "I assumed that everybody knew their place."

In her nearly twenty-five years as assistant, then associate, dean for academic affairs, Phyllis effectively rode the wave of growing acceptance of women in the university. Her experience in many ways echoed that of Jewish academics like myself, who benefited from what for a brief time was an outbreak of philo-Semitism.

Phyllis, like other successful participants in that first feminist onslaught, brought unique skills to her job. She had the emollient and persuasive gifts of discourse and strategy that are often part of the arsenal of women making their way in the world of men. Suasion—the ability to convince overly assertive academics that they may best attain their ends through patience and compromise—and a high disdain for the straitjacket mentality of the bureaucracy were her stocks in trade. And a booming trade it became, as the demands on the university by state, society, and faculty escalated. It was not easy to be an effective non-faculty administrator in a status-obsessed, faculty-run institution. But for much of her Arts and Sciences clientele, she became the go-to person for their wants and needs. [Plate 14]

At the same time—and this was part of her strength—she had an able academic's capacity to observe wisely and well the policies she did so much to implement. Chief among these was Harvard's influential core curriculum, for whose creation she was the principal staff person. She wrote *Getting at the Core: Curricular Reform at Harvard* (Harvard University Press, 1982) about the core curriculum, in particular its political and intellectual sources, from the perspective of a centrally placed participant-observer.

Not all was sweetness and light: she was a closer as well as an expediter. Asked once what precisely it was that she did, she replied, "After the dean passes over a battlefield, I go around and shoot the wounded." A more concrete illustration: the barely functioning Sanskrit Department thought to strengthen its hand by seeking a new position in Bengali. The crux of its pitch: did the administration realize that there were more than 200 million people who spoke Bengali? In her most earnest administrative manner, Phyllis asked, "Isn't that enough?" This put an admittedly temporary halt to the proposal.

In 2006, some years after her retirement, the Harvard Alumni Association gave Phyllis its Harvard Medal for exceptional service to the university. The citation spoke of her as an "invaluable colleague, counselor, and planner for almost twenty-five years to deans of the faculty of Arts and Sciences," who "strengthened Harvard at its core by your devotion to the academic life of the University." More pungently, the program observed, "Phyllis Keller is not your ordinary Medal candidate, but if one takes extraordinary service to Harvard seriously, it would be difficult to find an individual more worthy of recognition. For over twenty years she was 'principal custodian of quality in the Faculty of Arts and Sciences,' according to a dean of FAS. She was widely recognized as tough, good-humored, terribly smart, and entirely devoted to the academic side of FAS administration." (In the spirit of Phyllis, if not of the auspicious occasion, she responded sotto voce when Derek Bok gave her the medal: "I accept it posthumously.") [Plate 15]

Rounding out the family were our then all-but-obligatory two children, idyllically consisting of a daughter, Robin, and a son, Jon. It would take a major exercise in self-restraint to avoid the cute sayings and affecting anecdotes that attach themselves like kudzu grass to a parental narrative. I have manfully tried to live up to that ultimate expression of parental self-denial. Alas: no go.

But I'll limit myself to two vignettes, readily justifiable (to me) because they foretold qualities that would come to the fore when our children came to live their own lives in their own times.

Daughter Robin, aged two-plus, rushes into our garden apartment, face flushed from the exertions of the playground. She stops, transfixed by what her parents are watching on TV: a production of Richard III, more particularly the bloody height of the Battle of Bosworth Field that marks the end of Richard. She takes in the butchery, and authoritatively pronounces: "No hitting! No fighting! No pushing down!" Here is the first intimation that she will evolve into a corporate reorganization attorney with a formidable capacity to bring contending interests to mutually productive compromise.

Son Jon, at age eight or so, is hard at work on a coloring book with scenes from American history in outline, designed for rough-hewn coloring by not very tutored little fingers. Jon fastens on the affecting scene of Thomas Alva Edison seated at a table, staring at his electric light experiment. But instead of dutifully filling in the appropriate parts with inappropriate colors, he draws a balloon over Edison's head, and within the balloon inserts a glowing light bulb.

I showed this to a historian friend, who snorted: "He'll never be a historian; he's got it all wrong. It should be a candle." From there Jon went on to his life career as a television-radio-print political journalist, his stock in trade an idiosyncratically independent and original take on public affairs and the men who conduct them. It does indeed seem that character is destiny.

As academics' offspring in an aspiring time, our children not surprisingly wound up in posh Cambridge-Boston schools. In part because Jon's precocity pushed him too fast up the public school escalator, he and his sister first attended Cambridge's Shady Hill School, and then, for high school, the Commonwealth School in Boston.

This may have been inevitable; it may or may not have been wise. The mid-to-late 1960s and early 1970s were not an ideal time to expose one's offspring to the hothouse, with-it atmosphere of such schools in one of the fever spots of the gathering counterculture. Shady Hill turned over its fifth grade, in the year our daughter was part of it, to a member of a good (i.e., old) Cambridge family who had little else to commend him. He subjected his charges to a year of what he no doubt regarded as uplifting immersion in the ways of Native Americans, in place of ancient Greece, the traditional core theme of the year. The benefits this brought to a better understanding of Native Americans were at best a wash. But it was all too clear that for the intellectual development of the students, the year was a washout.

This romp through the swamps of political correctness was eerily replayed for our daughter when she was in the Commonwealth School. Commonwealth was not a venerable Boston institution. But under the headmastership of Charles Merrill, the brother of poet James Ingram Merrill and, more germane, the well-heeled son of stockbroker Charles E. Merrill of Merrill Lynch, the school won a reputation as a successful blend of enlightened student-rearing (the only fixed rule: no roller skating in the hallways) and a rigorous curriculum. But the times they were a-changin'. As our daughter arrived, the school's medieval history course was replaced by a somewhat differently conceived course in Mexican history.

The social surround of these school years was, of course, the well-known liberation of the Aquarian Age. The inflations of sex and drugs were the most conspicuous expressions of the new freedom. These had been far less conspicuous forms of behavior in our adolescence; they appeared to flourish most in society's upper and lower social fringes. (But recent opinion to the contrary notwithstanding, our generation was not unaware of the character and emoluments of the sexual act.) Now they became vested with political meaning, personal statements linked to the civil rights and anti-Vietnam War movements.

We had trouble with much of this, though not with the civil rights movement until it morphed into black nationalism. A number of our peers underwent a similar evolution, in good part I think for psychological as well as policy reasons. As I observed before, many of our generation had a large investment in an idealized view of academic life: colleagues and selves engaging in a search, if not for truth, at least for greater understanding: teachers seeking to convey as best they could their fields of expertise to students eager to hear what they had to say. A similar idealized view prevailed about our country, which we saw as recapitulating its epochal fight against German and Japanese fascism by responding to the challenge of Communism, and at the same time finally beginning to make significant progress against its greatest domestic faults: racial and gender discrimination.

It was not easy to be brushed aside as outmoded, deluded apologists for a brutal, racist nation devoting itself to the bloody repression of the Third World at home and abroad. But ours was hardly the only reaction to the New Age. The mirror image of our outrage at the violence and anti-Americanism of the counter-culture was the similarly psychological and sociological need of a number of our middle-age peers to identify (in their dress, their behavior, their beliefs) with the ideologically committed young.

Why did our children ultimately identify with, rather than rebel against, our squareness? To some degree they *did* rebel. They were of their time in dress and appearance, though to a far lesser extent in behavior. Compared to many of their counter-parts in the families we knew and lived among, they were odd persons out. An instance: it became the custom of a number of the *jeunesse dorée* at the Commonwealth School to gather outside the school early in the morning one day a week and decide, through collective decision-making (as was usually the case with such exercises in participatory democracy, no doubt in fact manipulated by the cadres), to grace a section of Boston with their presence by a stroll named, in the then-fashionable patois,

Citywalk. Our children and a few other deviants stood at the fringes of this communal wallow, waited for the decision, and then set out in the opposite direction: Counterwalk.

Their college experiences only deepened this predilection, assisted no doubt by the passion and prevalence of our distaste for what was going on in the surrounding culture. Robin went off to Harvard in 1971, when the full force of the counterculture had broken over that citadel of tradition. In proper New Age spirit, the communal bathrooms on each floor of her first-year dorm were gender-integrated. Since we lived only a block away, Robin coped well enough. But for most, that was a bit much, and this application of Liberty Hall soon faded away.

The new spirit affected more primal (psychological, if not physiological) urges as well. The residential pattern in her newly gender-integrated Radcliffe Quad dorm came to be freshman girl, senior boy who had not yet hooked up with a girl, freshman girl . . . This was not an easy milieu for sensitive, complex young people. By Thanksgiving the senior boy who lived directly above Robin's room had hanged himself.

In her sophomore year Robin and two others of her class were admitted into the Classics division of the college's History and Literature program. By their junior year all had dropped out, disillusioned by the pedagogy of the professor of Greek and Roman history, who appeared to think that bibliography was the "open sesame" for undergraduates in the field. Later, Robin had a graduate student tutor who acted in the belief that her primary educational responsibility was to type the chapters of his dissertation.

She drifted into the Government department. There her desire to write a senior thesis on the place of religion in classical political thought found no faculty takers. Finally, a history professor friend of the family offered to supervise her thesis. But it would have to be on a subject of his choosing: the legal system prevailing under the Terror during the French Revolution. She wrote a creditable study of one of the Terror's tribunals, but made the mistake of analogizing what went on there to Stalin's purge trials. One of the readers (all were graduate students) dismissed her thesis as of no value since it was "locked into the framework of Anglo-Saxon liberalism." This experience may not have been totally disconnected from her post-law school career in corporate reorganization law and her fervent Republicanism.

Son Jon responded more favorably to the Dionysian world of his time. But he too experienced the rough edges of Liberty Hall without a servant class to pick up after the inmates. He went to Columbia, despite a suggestive encounter when he applied there. His interviewer (of course an undergraduate) asked him, pro forma, why he wanted to come to Columbia. Raised in the bosom of a family more than cursorily dedicated to the Great American Songbook as filtered through the magical voice of Ella Fitzgerald, he answered, "Why, Rodgers and Hart went here." His inquisitor of course had not heard of them.

We dutifully took him, on a broiling Labor Day weekend, to move into his freshman dorm. Phyllis, wise to the wayward ways and mean-spirited means of the Columbia bureaucracy, saw to it that all, and more, than was humanly possible was done to get his documents, fees, etc., in order before he arrived. Nevertheless the lines were endless, his keys and room assignment were in limbo, and when we finally got him to his quarters, it turned out that the cell had been inhabited during the summer by a student who painted every paintable surface black. Of course it had been untouched since the previous inmate left some weeks before, and the milk and other perishable foodstuffs had had ample time to revert to a state of nature.

It soon became clear that this was among the milder aspects of the *Lord of the Flies* subculture that had descended on much of American academe. Early on in his freshman year, Jon and a friend went to a rock concert in the Hunter College auditorium. It soon turned out that they were the only whites in a crowd of six hundred or so. They were quickly taught the error of their ways: beaten up, their watches, wallets, and overcoats liberated.

After a year Jon abandoned Columbia and, indeed, New York. He rationalized his decision in typically elliptical fashion: he could not, he said, live in a city where a plain pizza cost $9.50. He transferred to Brandeis, where his father, on the faculty, was strategically placed to do not very much for him. But at least the violence level in Waltham did not match that of the Upper West Side in New York. He spent his last two college years rooming in town with a black high school friend who was at Harvard, also from a family with square parents unattracted by the Age of Aquarius.

To grow up in those years was not unlike spending one's formative time in a boot camp: you were either crippled or strengthened by the experience. Robin went off to law school and a career in corporate bankruptcy law, a particularly nuts-and-bolts field of endeavor with only a thin carapace of academic theorizing attached to it. Jon (who when he was about eleven years old told us that when he grew up he wanted to communicate, and didn't much care what it was that he was communicating) headed even more single-mindedly into radio broadcasting. In time he gravitated to political commentary in newspapers and magazines, on radio and television, and in a book, *The Bluest State* (St. Martin's Press, 2007), that eviscerated the Democratic political culture of Massachusetts. Most definitely they were survivors, not victims, of the times in which their lives took form.

CHAPTER SIX

The Late Middle Ages

MY EXPERIENCE of the 1960s and 1970s as a participant, and my reading of them as a historian, is not suffused in the warm, cuddly afterglow that one so often finds in baby boomer retrospection. I don't deny that altruism and idealism were present in the mindset of many (by no means all) of the *engagés* of the sixties. But these higher values were inextricably entangled with less elevated drives.

What I regard as perhaps the prime cause of the cultural transformation that burst on our society in the 1960s was the stunning change in the relative size and rate of growth of the major age cohorts. Let me make my point by a table that shows the percentage rate of growth between census years of "Children" (five to thirty-four years old) and "Parents" (thirty-five to fifty-four years old) from 1900 to 1970. (See Table 1 on the following page.)

The cohort of "parents" increased at a faster rate than "children" from 1900 to 1950. It is not surprising that during those years traditional norms of parental authority, and the market dominance of the parental group, prevailed even in the face of

TABLE 1

	"Children"	"Parents"
1900–1910	17%	30%
1910–1920	10	20
1920–1930	9	17
1930–1940	− 2	12
1940–1950	9	24
1950–1960	31	6
1960–1970	16	− 1
1970–1980	− 18	20
1980–1990	− 6	24
1990–2000	11	16
2000–2006	5	13

Source: Data from U.S. Census Bureau.

socially destabilizing technological changes such as movies and the automobile.

By the same token, from 1950 to 1970 the rate of increase of "children" suddenly, and far, outstripped a stagnant parental cohort. Cultural mores and market trends shifted to reflect, and care and feed, that group. The result was "the sixties" (stretching into the seventies), with all the resonance of social and cultural upheaval that label signifies. After that the imbalance sharply lessened and the predominance of the young began to slow, with consequences such as a decline in crime and the vogue of retro revivals and sequels in popular culture.

The unprecedented upset of the generational balance in the 1960s fostered a comparably dramatic change in social experience. The generation that came of age during the twenty years after the end of World War II was not only uniquely larger than that of its parents, but was shielded as none had been before from the scourges of economic want, disease, and war.

The twin facts of relative size and relative affluence led to a truncation between the generations with no parallel in the past. The boomers were numerous enough, and well-heeled enough, to seize the attention of the big media and commercial marketing companies and to support a popular culture of clothes, movies, music, and taste directed at them. Given their flood of numbers, there took root social attitudes and values, a life style, even a language that was theirs alone. Under the prodding of spokesmen and demagogues quick to seize on their numerical weight, the boomers became a social, economic, and, increasingly, a political force to be reckoned with.

Most notably in those protected enclaves of their generation, the colleges and universities, the boomers of the West posed a challenge to social and cultural (and, less so, to political) authority. But this was not a development unique to the United States, or even to the affluent West. The Red Guards of Mao's China were not always fully controlled handmaidens of the dictator; they may have echoed but were far more violent than alienated American and European youths. Nor did the French and British student rebels imitate their American counterparts by dwelling on civil rights and Vietnam. Yet for all these differences, there were common denominators of alienation from the past, parents, and traditional mores, plus a messianic sense of a social mission to change everything.

Of course there was more to the sixties than this generational glitch. The violent white Southern resistance to the civil rights revolution, and the grounds for opposition to the Vietnam War, were real enough. But when set against the horrors wrought by

Hitler and Stalin, by Mao and Pol Pot, even causes as justifiable as these might well seem to be of a lesser order of magnitude.

And the boomer reaction not infrequently evolved into True Believers Going Too Far. Thus, the Martin Luther King-civil rights Freedom Marchers' appeal to the better natures of Americans was corrupted by the violence and extremism of the Black Panthers and the urban riots of the late sixties. These did great harm to, though they did not derail, the slow but inexorable transformation of white thinking about race.

A very similar evolution occurred in the protest movement against the Vietnam War. Clean for Gene (McCarthy) and the Bobby Kennedy campaign foundered on the murder of RFK by a Palestinian militant and the Chicago Democratic Convention riots of 1968. The turn to violence by the Weathermen and their like fostered not the transformation of Americans into enemies of a corrupt, imperialistic Amerika, but to the election, and overwhelming re-election, of Richard Nixon.

Thus our times. What about our lives? How profoundly were we altered by the sea changes in the public sphere?

These grand events may have radicalized a number of members of the boomer generation and a (smaller) portion of my generation. But Phyllis and I and, if the political reaction of the 1970s and 1980s is any indication, a large number of our peers had a very different reaction. I voted for Hubert Humphrey in 1968 and, in a last, ill-considered, gasp of my New Deal-Democratic antecedence, for Jimmy Carter in 1976. After 1968, Phyllis underwent no such liberal/Democratic episode.

Living in Cambridge and being part of the academic community at this time was in many respects an out-of-body experience. It was not easy to make your way in a subculture whose public and private musings embodied what seemed a prime example of that (sadly) recurring historical phenomenon, the fear and madness of crowds.

Many of those around us regarded President Lyndon Johnson and the Vietnam War as monstrosities all but unmatched in history, except perhaps for the bombing of Dresden, the Japanese relocation camps, Hiroshima/Nagasaki, and, of course, the Holocaust. I remember chatting one mid-sixties day with Federal District Judge Charles Wyzanski, who along with Harvard Law professor Paul Freund was a perennial Cambridge (but not elsewhere) favorite candidate for the Supreme Court. In the course of a *tour d'horizon* of the state of the nation, Wyzanski concluded that there was only one answer to our problems: "Someone has to assassinate the president." Of course this was only Cambridge hyperbole. But coming as it did a few years after the JFK tragedy, it did seem . . . excessive.

It struck us as bizarre that so many well-educated academics, snug in the security blanket of tenure, were inclined to anti-Americanism and indifferent to Communist totalitarianism. After all, this was barely a generation after the defeat of the German and Japanese fascists and the revelation of Stalin's crimes, and bracketed by the great Mao-induced Chinese famine of 1959–61 and Pol Pot's Cambodian genocide in the late 1970s.

One might have thought that these not-minor danger signals would have stirred a certain suspicion of social engineering designed by policy intellectuals and racist/Marxist theory and implemented by an interventionist state. But ideological love affairs, or at least intense friendships, with the totalitarian flavor of the year (Castro's Cuba, Ho Chi Minh's Viet Cong, Nicaragua's Sandinistas, Mao's Permanent Revolution) were the recurring disposition of many academics in our Cambridge ambit.

Our political and social attitudes, quite consistent from the earliest days of post-childhood awareness in the 1940s to our adult maturity in the 1960s, were profoundly altered by the end of what historian Richard Hofstadter called "a slum of a decade." As the promise of the New Frontier and the Great Society gave way to what were for us the darker goals of the New Left, our social world underwent a reconfiguration. Old friendships sustained by more or less shared values began to erode as we went our separate political and social ways. We fell into what in retrospect seems like a circle-the-wagons stance, turning away from those with whom we no longer saw eye to eye, clinging more closely to the like-minded.

This was an evolution furthered not only by social and political predilections but by the tone and tenor of everyday life. Crime brought more closely home the disorder that the Vietnam War and political assassination highlighted on the higher levels of public policy and social-political ideology.

Our son once was robbed at knifepoint in Cambridge Common at mid-day. When Phyllis reported this to the police, she was reassured that if it had gotten more violent, the undercover drugs officer at the Common no doubt would have intervened; but meanwhile he had to maintain his cover. Within walking distance in our reasonably affluent neighborhood, in short order a young woman was murdered in an apartment house and the wife of a Harvard faculty member was dragged into an adjacent park and killed. The nearby Radcliffe dormitories became bastions of ID-card, locked-door security. Warning devices, instructions to act cautiously, and a conspicuous police presence burgeoned in the suddenly insecure spaces between dorms and classroom buildings.

With cause, "Take back the streets!" became a new feminist battle cry. Meanwhile, the large presence of street people—anarchists, dropouts, druggies—became an everyday presence in our lives. For years after the Iran hostage crisis started in November 1979, a graffito, untouched by the authorities, exhorted passersby on the Common: "Hang the hostages!"

There were, both at Brandeis and at Harvard, old Lefties (more likely to have been disciples of Trotsky than of Stalin) who reacted viscerally to the anti-democratic behavior and yen for violence among student radicals and the fringes of the New Left. With its Jewish base and offbeat campus culture, Brandeis by the time I got there had become a repository of at least one representative of every left-wing splinter group of the mid-twentieth century. There was neo-Stalinist Herbert Marcuse, gravitating (in theory alone, of course) to Maoism and Third Worldism as a mountain stream gushes downhill. There was the quiet (I thought quietly sinister) mathematical logician Jean van Heijenoort, who was Trotsky's personal secretary from 1932 to 1939. (In 1986 he was bizarrely murdered in Mexico City, where Trotsky met his end, by his estranged fourth wife.) There were at least a couple of Shakmanites (adherents of an exotic Trotskyite spinoff) cutting each other dead in the Faculty Club. There was social democrat John Roche of the Politics Department, a co-founder and former chairman of Americans for Democratic Action, special adviser to President Johnson, and supporter of the Vietnam War (which condemned him to virtual academic non-personhood); and my colleague Marvin Meyers, Trotskyite-turned academic-turned bitter enemy of the New Left, which he saw corrupting his academic utopianism as Stalinism had corrupted his social utopianism.

Harvard had become a place of refuge for "White Berkeleyans" Seymour Martin Lipset and Nathan Glazer, who fled that radicalized place to teach sociology, much as their anti-Bolshevik White Russian analogues came to drive taxicabs in Paris. Another ex-Berkeleyan, economic historian Henry Rosovsky, who brought Phyllis into the Harvard administration, was contemporaneous with, but not really part of, this circle.

A number of Harvard acquaintances shared our heavy emotional and ideological investment in the academic ideal now challenged by the New Left, and responded much as we did. With our closest friends, Harvard economic historian (and another Berkeley émigré) David Landes and his wife, Sonia, we shared as well a compatibility of the sort upon which any close relationship depends. And there were Constitutional law scholar Robert McCloskey and political scientists James Q. Wilson and Edward Banfield, who brought a Chicago-hewn skeptical conservatism to this intellectual mix. Wilson observed that he had been closely involved with a number of major American institutions in the course of his adult life, including the United States Navy, the University of Chicago, and Harvard; and that Harvard stood nowhere near the top when it came to fostering free inquiry. Banfield was particularly insightful (in my view) when he observed that sometimes the best public policy was: "Don't just do something; stand there."

The companionship of these people lessened our sense of isolation from the main currents of the academy. An instance lodges in my memory of that time. Phyllis and I paid one of our infrequent visits to New York in the early 1970s. Who to see? The only people left with whom we could spend time comfortably, we decided, were publisher Irving Kristol and his wife Bea (aka historian Gertrude Himmelfarb) and Columbia historian Eric McKitrick. We called the McKitricks, and they asked us to dinner. In due course there arrived their other invitees, presumably among the few people left with whom they could socialize: Bea and Irv Kristol.

EXCURSUS
The Song Is Ended But the Melody Lingers On

I can think of no better way to convey my sense of the gulf that separated so many of my mid-twentieth-century contemporaries from our successors than that lodestone of our culture, popular music: more particularly, its lyrics. In the long run it was the ongoing, inexorable process of changing cultural taste, more than the in-many-ways transient glitch of the politics of the sixties, that marked this generational divide.

In November 2004, *Rolling Stone* magazine bestowed on its readers a list of "The 500 Greatest Songs of All Time." With the modesty characteristic of the magazine and its generation, "Like a Rolling Stone" topped the list. The less self-servingly titled "Satisfaction" came next—though the favored version was by (who else?) The Rolling Stones.

The Greatest Songs of All Time turned out to be a generationally challenged concept. Only one song dated back to the dim past of the 1940s, and that was the hardly imperishable "I'm So Lonesome I Could Cry" (performed, needless to say, by The Rolling Stones). The great majority of the All-Time Hit Parade was contemporary with *Rolling Stone's* glory days in the 1960s and 1970s. As the magazine, and its founders, got older, the Greatest Songs began to die out: only three emerged to grace our culture after 2000.

Besides being a revealing instance of the degree to which the Caring Generation cared most about itself, *Rolling Stone's* navel-gazing brings out in high relief my sense of belonging to a time-bound cultural milieu.

Popular song as much as anything distinguishes modern America's kaleidoscopic sequence of generations one from the other. None of MY list of the "Greatest Songs of All Time" made it onto *Rolling Stone's* roll of honor. I am as firmly in thrall as any rock fan to the corpus of five tunesmiths and their lyricists: the ground-breaking teams of Jerome Kern and his lyricists P.G. Wodehouse and Dorothy Fields; Irving Berlin and *his* lyricist, Irving Berlin; and the Big Three of George and Ira Gershwin, Richard Rodgers and Lorenz Hart/Oscar Hammerstein II, and Cole Porter, another lyrics do-it-yourselfer.

Of course the great bulk of the songs embedded in the memory lobes of my generation are prime contenders in the Mediocrity Sweepstakes. Clunky words and a June-moon lack of originality too often coincided with an easy, female-degrading sexism:

> Sentimental baby, sweet and gentle baby
> Just the way a baby ought to be . . .*

But the songs that most powerfully shaped so much of my and many of my peers' perception of the world, and which persist in our culture with a staying power that tells us how special they are (in Irving Berlin's words, they keep coming back like a song), were the work of the Big Five, the core of the Great American Songbook.

---

*"Sentimental Baby." Threesome Music. 1960.

There was much more to these songs than clever variations of boy-meets-girl. Let's begin with who their creators were and the social impulses that gave life to their work. All but Porter and Wodehouse were Jewish. And though Porter was a Yale-degreed Episcopalian, he was gay at a time when that fact of life was not (to put it mildly) socially acceptable. He told Richard Rodgers that early on he fastened on the high road to success: "Simplicity itself. I'll write Jewish music."

Rodgers, Hammerstein, and Kern came from comfortable, assimilated families. Berlin and the Gershwins were straight out of the immigrant ghetto. Yet they had a shared impulse to seize not only the opportunities but the substance of mainstream native-born, affluent-educated white Protestant American life. And in varying ways they responded to the call for social justice that was part of both Jewish tradition and the modern urban America in which they lived. In short, they gave voice to urges that resonated strongly with my generation.

There were, I think, three themes that made these songs so transfixing to many of us. One was a mix of American patriotism and social conscience, stoked by a racial tolerance that for the time was cutting-edge. Another was a cultural aspiration that took such forms as delight in wordplay and wit, in the texture of the American urban scene, and sometimes (for so popular a medium) surprisingly sophisticated references to Western history and culture. The third was a rejection of the banality that for so long typified the popular music (and much else beside) treatment of that hardy perennial, the interplay of boys and girls.

Here a problem appears, of the sort that is grist for the historian's mill. The great songs of the early and mid-twentieth century catered to an audience far less college-educated than is the case today. Yet Jerome Kern's lyricists P.G. Wodehouse and Dorothy

Fields, to say nothing of Ira Gershwin, Lorenz Hart, and Porter, wrote sharp-edged, often witty, culture-drenched verse that yet appealed to large musical comedy audiences and even larger movie and radio cohorts. And while Irving Berlin may have had the most common touch, it remains something of a wonder that in that bias-ridden age the most conspicuously immigrant-Jewish of the lot should have been America's songster.

It can be argued that to be responsive to tuneful melodies and clever verbal variations of the love game hardly required the benefits of higher education. But the wordsmiths often turned the conventional love song inside out, treating the core boy-girl story with irony and wit. Thus Ginger Rogers rebuking Fred Astaire for "A Fine Romance" (Kern and Fields) in Hollywood's *Swing Time* (1936):

> A fine romance with no quarrels
> With no insults and all morals . . .*

Or the knockabout Rodgers and Hart "I Wish I Were in Love Again" (1937):

> You don't know that I felt good
> When we up and parted . . .
> I sleep all night, appetite and health restored.
> You don't know how much I'm bored!†

It is conventional current cant that only with the liberation of the sixties was the popular culture freed to explore sex with

---

*Rogers, G., perf. "A Fine Romance." *Swing Time*. T.B. Harms Co. 1936.
†"I Wish I Were in Love Again." Chappell & Co., Inc./Williamson Music, Inc. 1937.

blinkers off. Yet it appears that procreation was not unknown even in the pre-Aquarian Dark Ages. The Great American Songbook showed an awareness that there was more to love than mooning and spooning. Thus the Gershwins' "Do It Again" (1922), with kissing a surrogate for you-know-what:

> My lips just ache
> To have you take
> The kiss that's waiting for you.
> You know if you do
> You won't regret it.
> Come and get it*
> . . .

It is worth comparing this with a recent song that bears the same title:

> Let me do what I want to do with you
> Let me tie you down and pick you up and
> Flip you all around
> . . .
> Wake me up in the morning by pouring
> Honey on my body and licking it off . . .†

Far from being sexually super-charged, contemporary youth appears to need considerable inducement to get charged at all.

Social conscience is another supposed void in the Songbook world. A PBS documentary on Woody Guthrie, replayed at what seems like twenty-minute intervals, observes that only with the

---

*"Do It Again." New World Music/Wb Music Corp. 1922.
†"Do It Again." Universal Motown Records, a division of UMG Recordings, Inc. 2002.

appearance of the iconic "This Land Is Your Land" did social awareness enter onto the hitherto indifferent landscape of American popular song.

That isn't quite right. Of course it wouldn't be difficult to match or surpass "This Land's" faux-folksy lyrics:

> This land is your land, this land is my land
> From California to the New York Island*

Guthrie wrote the song in 1940 as a counter to Irving Berlin's "God Bless America" during that (best-forgotten) interlude of the Nazi-Soviet Pact of 1939–41, when Popular Front anti-Nazi patriotism was suspended—until the Soviet Union was invaded in June 1941. In fact there had been other glimmers of social light. During the segregationist nadir of the early twentieth century, Songbook writers reached out across the racial barrier. Irving Berlin's "Alexander's Ragtime Band" (1911) added substantially to the luster of a black musical form. Jerome Kern's *Show Boat* (1927) brought interracial love to Broadway; Irving Berlin's "Suppertime" (1933) dealt poignantly with the travails of the single mother of a black family:

> How'll I keep explainin'
> When they ask me where he's gone?
> . . .
> How can I be thankful
> When they start to thank the Lord?
> Lord!†

---

*"This Land Is Your Land." TRO-Ludlow Music, Inc. (BMI). 1940.
†"Suppertime." Irving Berlin Music Company. 1933.

And the Gershwins' *Porgy and Bess* (1935) made love and tragedy in a black community the stuff of what arguably is the greatest American musical achievement.

Cole Porter's "Love for Sale" and Rodgers and Hart's "Ten Cents a Dance," appearing in the Depression year of 1930, took up not the evil of private property and the romance of Communism, but the exploitation of women:

> Love for sale,
> Appetizing young love for sale.
> Love that's fresh and still unspoiled,
> Love that's only slightly soiled,
> Love for sale.*

> Ten cents a dance
> That's what they pay me.
> Gosh, how they weigh me down!
> . . .
> Fighters and sailors and bowlegged tailors
> Can pay for their ticket and rent me!
> Butchers and barbers and rats from the harbors
> Are sweethearts my good luck has sent me.†

Even that sellout Irving Berlin, whose "God Bless America" and "White Christmas" reflected the patriotism and sentimentality of the Second World War, showed in his 1937 "Slumming on Park Avenue" a rudimentary class awareness, though of course not up to Guthrie's agitpropriety:

> Let's go slumming, take me slumming,
> Let's go slumming on Park Avenue.
> . . .

---

*"Love for Sale." Wb Music Corp. 1930.
†"Ten Cents a Dance." Wb Music Corp./Williamson Music, Inc. 1930.

Let's go smelling where they're dwelling,
Sniffing everything the way they do;

. . .

Let's go slumming, nose thumbing, on Park Avenue.*

But it was the mix of wit, history, and a passion for the cultural artifacts of an urban America into which these artists—and then later I—came of age that most richly colored their songs and my response to them. In this they played a role similar to S.J. Perelman and the Hollywood films of the 1930s and 1940s: assisting my post-immigrant generation in the serious business of acculturation to an America alive with possibility. If the major impulse of today's purveyors of popular culture is to give voice to alienation from the larger society, precisely the opposite goal was the most compelling cultural theme in my formative decades.

Change and modernity were not necessarily celebrated, as Cole Porter made clear in "Anything Goes" (1934):

In olden days a glimpse of stocking
Was looked on as something shocking,
But now, God knows, Anything Goes.
Good authors who once knew better words
Now only use four letter words.
Writing prose, Anything Goes.†

At the same time, Porter and his fellow-songsters loved to flaunt references to a booming, blooming world of history,

---

*"Slumming on Park Avenue." Irving Berlin Music Company. 1937.
†"Anything Goes." Wb Music Corp. 1934.

exotic places, culture popular and elite, and all the infinitely var-
iegated stuff of modern America, even in Depression-ridden
1934:

> You're the top!
> You're the Coliseum.
> You're the top!
> You're the Louvre Museum.
> You're a melody from a symphony by Strauss.
> You're a Bendel bonnet
> A Shakespeare sonnet,
> You're Mickey Mouse.*

Ira Gershwin had similar inclinations:

> They all laughed at Christopher Columbus
> When he said the world was round.
> They all laughed when Edison recorded sound.
> They all laughed at Wilbur and his brother
> When they said that man could fly;
> They told Marconi
> Wireless was a phony;
> It's the same old cry†

The American language itself was another feature of these
songs. The Gershwins' "'S Wonderful" (1927) celebrated that
mainstay of popular speech, the contraction:

> 'S wonderful! 'S marvelous!
> You should care for me!

---

*"You're the Top." Wb Music Corp. 1934.
†"They All Laughed." George Gershwin Music/Wb Music Corp./Ira Gershwin Music/Wb Music Corp. 1937.

'S awful nice! 'S paradise!
'S what I love to see!*

And their "Let's Call the Whole Thing Off" (1937) played on variants of pronunciation:

You say eether and I say eyether,
You say neether and I say nyether

. . .

You like potayto and I like potahto,
You like tomayto and I like tomahto†

Among the latter-day musical comedy inheritors of the Great American Songbook are the widely popular, resolutely Pop Culture Andrew Lloyd Webber (*Cats, Les Miserables, Jesus Christ Superstar, Man of La Mancha*) and the not-so-sweet voice of the post-modern sensibility Stephen Sondheim (*Sweeney Todd, Sunday in the Park with George*).

There are links between my Big Five and these Next Two. Webber was a devotee of Richard Rodgers, Sondheim was the protégé of lyricist Oscar Hammerstein. But Webber is capable of a maudlin kitsch that Rodgers and Hammerstein at their soupiest didn't quite reach. Wit, sophistication, exploration of the nuances of the larger culture: those hallmarks of the best of the Great American Songbook have little or no place in Webber's bland verse.

But the yearning remains. Revivals of Songbook musicals from *Show Boat* to *My Fair Lady* come regularly. Most are pale and

---

*"'S Wonderful." Wb Music Corp. 1927.
†"Let's Call the Whole Thing Off." George Gershwin Music/Wb Music Corp./ Ira Gershwin Music/Wb Music Corp. 1937.

bloodless, testimony to the fact that the cultural moment that gave them life is gone. Case in point: the 1988 revival of Kern's *Show Boat* couldn't cope with the opening line of "Ol' Man River" ("Niggers all work on de Mississippi") and replaced it with the anodyne "Colored folk work . . ."

Sondheim is in even greater cultural-ideological opposition to his predecessors. His appeal is to the prevailing style of intellectuals and their cultural fellow-travelers of the past half century: a visceral anti-Americanism (the American Dream transposed into the American Nightmare); an inbred distaste for what he regards as bourgeois taste and morality; a rejection of wit or wordplay in his lyrics, and lyricism in his music, that faithfully reflects the mind-set of the more pretentious elements of the prevailing culture. Prominent in the Sondheim Hit Parade is "A Little Priest," in which the principal gourmets in *Sweeney Todd* discourse on the culinary qualities of various human courses. (To my taste, a little priest goes a long way.)

Sondheim wins the plaudits of "serious" critics and other standard-setters but less so of audiences. Here again there is a paradox. Sondheim's auditors are far more likely to be college-educated and socially sophisticated than their predecessors. Yet his songs abjure the wit and wordplay that so captivated the less culturally privileged audiences of the Gershwins-Porter-Rodgers-and-Hart era.

Why should this be? One obvious answer is that Americans in the first half of the twentieth century, immigrant and native-born alike, were gripped by the impulse to assimilate, improve, raise themselves from their agricultural-industrial-immigrant backgrounds. Their late twentieth-century counterparts, born into a relatively affluent, middle-class (as opposed to agrarian/

working-class) country, are more drawn to the high-end cultural goods of alienation and anomie.

This is theory; now a piece of praxis. Some years ago I met with the gifted satirist Tom Lehrer to discuss an American Academy of Arts and Sciences program to present some of the highlights of the Great American Songbook. Things went swimmingly until I expressed a preference for the best of the Songbook over Sondheim. Lehrer exploded with indignation: Sondheim, he insisted, was in a class by himself. Clearly we looked at things from opposite sides of a cultural divide.

The artists of the Songbook were not the only formative voices in twentieth-century popular culture. Jazz and blues spoke affectingly of the travails and yearnings of American blacks in the segregation era. Country music did the same for rural whites. And the political faux-folk songs of Guthrie, Pete Seeger, Bob Dylan, Joan Baez, and others have won a large youth audience for generations.

Most of all, rock-and-roll and the Beatles won, and kept, the boomers as they came of age. I can readily see how the beat and tone and substance of rock and its derivatives spoke to them as did the Songbook to my generation.

After the heady days of the sixties, the popular music taste of the younger generation took another turn. The idealistic-utopian tone of much sixties rock now became darker, more destructive and despairing. Not the pieties of the Popular Front but the we-have-nothing-to-lose mind-set of the black underclass set the tone. New genres followed each other in rapid-fire order: rap, hip-hop, metal, grunge, each with numerous spinoffs. Their message is a populist counterpart to the upscale, intellectualized nihilism of Sondheim.

This rotation of the pop-music wheel won a massive audience among the white middle-class, college-educated young: a classic case of *nostalgie de la boue*. Some of the chattering classes found high social and political meaning in these songs and lathered them in layers of significance not seen since the headier days of the Higher Jazz Criticism. Harvard found room for a hip-hop professor or two and its students benefited from courses such as Hip-hop America: Power, Politics, and the World; and Hip-hop World Order: Appropriation, Localization, and Racial Identification in Global Hip-hop.

I'm not qualified to pass on the musical worth of this (or any other) genre. And I'm quite prepared to believe that its wide appeal justifies its study. But as a wordsmith of sorts, I can respond to the lyrics of this music in terms of what it tells us about the generation that has grown up with it and the gulf of sensibility that lies between us.

The verbal substance of hip-hop, in this New Age of higher education, post-racism, women's equality, and Peace Now, is a recurrent triad: homophobia, misogyny, and racial violence. One observer says that it has descended from "clever rhymes and dance beats" to "personal, social and criminal corruption"—precisely as it took root in the larger world of white-suburban-college youth.

"No One's Iller" is the work of Eminem—improbable birth name Marshall Bruce Mathers II—who for a while was the Great White Hope of the otherwise black hip-hop industry. In this sense he is its Cole Porter: a white writing black music as Porter claimed to write Jewish songs. But his lyrics are hardly Porteresque:

> Drivin' down Van Dyke
> Get my dick sucked late at night by a fuckin' transvestite

Still on probation for stranglin' my boy Jason
Should be takin' my medication, it's 9 to 20 I'm facin'.
Last week this old man I had to blast
Cuz he tried to help me when my car was out of gas
Ripped this old lady, hung her neck by a hook
Didn't realize it was my grandmother 'til I checked her
  pocketbook.
Throwin' bottles at day care centers and yell "EVERYBODY
  GET OUT"!
My girl beat my ass and shot me in the back with a 2-piece
Cuz she found out I was havin' an affair with her 10-year-old
  niece.
No one, no one's iller than me.*

He's got a point.

And then there's "Fuck Tha Police," the *chef d'oeuvre* of the gangsta rap group N.W.A. (Niggers with Attitude), which made it to no. 417 on Rolling Stone's 500 Greatest. Copyright restrictions and a residual sense of decency limit what I put before you:

To the police I'm sayin fuck you punk
Readin my rights and shit, it's all junk†

We're not in Kansas anymore.

---

*"No One's Iller." Web Entertainment Records. 1997.
†"Fuck Tha Police." Ruthless Records/Priority Records. 1988.

CHAPTER SEVEN

After All

P HYLLIS AND I, along with the country, moved into a less adventurous, more sedate mode of existence as the fervid sixties and seventies gave way to the supposedly inner-directed eighties and nineties. These decades, in the self-serving construction of the boomer counterculture, were a time in which service to self—"greed" in the patois of the time—replaced a more idealistic, less self-obsessed mindset: that of the boomers.

My political-legal-regulatory-institutional brand of history remained marginal in a profession dominated by race-, class-, and gender-based social history and a postmodern-deconstructionist mode of discourse. Scholarly topics were now "projects," interest groups were "communities" (as in the "Jeremiad community" I heard referred to at an academic conference).

Just as I found social comfort in like-thinking fellow-academics, so did I find scholarly satisfaction in staying with the blend of political, administrative, and, increasingly, legal history that I had begun to explore in *The Life Insurance Enterprise* and *Affairs of State*. In the late 1970s I spent a year as a Liberal Arts Fellow at Harvard Law School, sopping up what legal technicalities I could without subjecting myself to the rigor of regular attendance at courses. I'm not sure how well that worked. But I did learn enough legalese (in words and thought) for two books of mine, *Regulating a New Economy* (1990) and *Regulating a New Society* (1994), to be accorded a reasonably respectful reception by legal history cognoscenti. (*Regulating a New Society* won the American Historical Association's Littleton-Griswold prize in legal history.) And I began to train graduate students in legal history who made something of a splash in that subject's admittedly confined precincts, among them William Novak at Chicago, Dirk Hartog at Princeton, and Michael Grossberg at Indiana.

In 1980 Harvard Business School historian Tom McCraw and I fielded a conference on the history of American economic regulation whose papers appeared in 1981 in *Regulation in Perspective: Historical Essays,* edited by McCraw. It made nobody's top ten list, but did win attention among those who devoted some of their waking hours to the subject.

Reasonably satisfying recognition came in the eighties and nineties. I was elected to the American Academy of Arts and Sciences, the Massachusetts Historical Society, and the British Academy. [Plate 16] With increasing frequency I found myself referred to in academic prints as "distinguished": I presume this is what comes before "the late." Family landmarks—our fortieth anniversary in 1993 [Plate 17], our fiftieth in 2003 [Plate 18]— were reminders that while I may have been progressing, so was time. As I approached the outer limits of middle age, my life as well as my times took on a more placid aspect.

At the same time my search for (or, better, tropistic leaning toward) a scholarly identity where disciplines conjoined, rather than where History had come in my view to fester, took another turn in the 1990s. I teamed up with my Brandeis Politics Department colleague Shep Melnick to teach a joint seminar to graduate students in history and political science, in which we sought to get them to merge the methods and insights of the two fields.

Our success was spotty. The grip of the disciplines is tenacious for both intellectual and sociological reasons. Nevertheless we extended this approach by running a conference at the Smithsonian's Woodrow Wilson International Center, showcasing what historians and political scientists had to say about some major concerns of American public policy: trade, social welfare, environmentalism, civil rights. The results appeared in *Taking Stock: American Government in the Twentieth Century* (1999).

The less than overwhelming response to the book was a tipoff that the academic (to say nothing of the political) world was not enthralled by an approach that was not strong in either (a) an economics-like grounding in theory or quantitative analysis or (b) a robust Left take on public policy issues. But no matter. By this time I had become inured to the fact that what I was doing was not in the mainstream of late twentieth-century academia.

Then seemingly extraneous events in Phyllis's and my careers moved me down a new path of history-writing. In the late 1990s, Phyllis decided that her energy in, and enthusiasm for, her tension-filled job was flagging. She had flourished in the deanships of Henry Rosovsky and economist A. Michael Spence. But under a new president, Neil Rudenstine, and a new dean, chemist Jeremy Knowles, the nature of her job and, indeed, of Harvard's bureaucratic culture began to change. In a nutshell, the old-boy/soft-shoe, mom-and-pop store ambience was giving way to a larger, more structured, more bureaucratized operation.

This was inevitable. But the sheer size and complexity of Harvard, the ever-encroaching demands of government regulation, and an ever more law-and-regulator-encrusted ambience made for an administrative environment less and less to her taste. And twenty-plus years of engagement in never-to-be-satisfied faculty care and feeding had its own cumulative erosive force.

So off she went in 1997 . . . to what? One possibility that arose as we discussed Whither Us? was a co-authored book: the ultimate test of the strength of a marriage. And what more at-hand subject than the history of modern Harvard?

Marvelously authoritative volumes on the seventeenth- and eighteenth-century university had been written by Samuel Eliot Morison, Harvard's colonial historian. Then he edited a pastiche of less satisfactory chapters on the departments and schools of nineteenth- and early twentieth-century Harvard. In 1936, the year of Harvard's Centennial celebration, he published *Three Centuries of Harvard*, a beguiling overview of the school's past. But it ended with the departure of Abbott Lawrence Lowell from the presidency in 1933.

Now, more than sixty years later, a great deal of Harvard history had passed under the bridge. And while several books took swipes of varying effectiveness at the more recent history of America's premier university, there had as yet been no attempt to write a large-scale account of Harvard's confrontation with modern times.

This we set out to do. After *Regulating a New Society*, my scholarly desk was clear. (I intended to write a third volume on American public life from 1900 to 1930 dealing with the political-legal-government infrastructure instead of policy. But I lost the drive to do so, and decided not to try to beat more life into a heavy-breathing horse.)

We worked up a description of the kind of book we hoped to write: as comprehensive as we could make it, and at the same time setting Harvard's modern history into the larger framework of what had been happening in recent times to American higher education and to the country at large. I made a pitch to the Spencer Foundation, which supported scholarship on education, and got a grant that allowed me to go on a half-time teaching schedule for three years: a not inappropriate exposure to the well-padded academic lifestyle that I needed to know about if I was going to write about America's wealthiest university.

So we got to work. Phyllis took the lead in setting up interviews with the dozens of Harvard movers, shakers, insiders, and foot soldiers upon whom we came to rely for the anecdotal and evidentiary flesh to attach to the bones of narrative and incident provided by printed and manuscript sources.

I found in the thousand boxes or so of the presidential papers of James Bryant Conant and Nathan Marsh Pusey, who ran the place from 1933 to 1971, a uniquely rich archive, not only as to how they conducted themselves and what they thought, but how Harvard worked as an institution. These were pre-computer, pre-Internet days, at a time when presidential authority was still something to be asserted, not concealed or apologized for.

This treasure trove enabled us to tackle every department in the Faculty of Arts and Sciences and all of the professional schools, as well as administration, fund-raising, alumni affairs, and the College (admissions, student culture, athletics, etc.).

What opened up to us was not only a wide window into the way the school functioned, but ample evidence of the central place that an often arrogant style had in the Harvard world. Just think of the personal and institutional self-assurance that lay behind the following rumination by Arts and Sciences Dean

McGeorge Bundy to President Pusey. He told Pusey that he wanted to appoint a physicist of great eminence, and had MIT's Victor Weisskopf in mind. Another potential catch at MIT was economist Paul Samuelson. But it was likely that Samuelson would want a university professorship: a bit above his station in academic life, Bundy thought. He conceded that MIT and Harvard had a gentlemen's agreement not to raid each other's faculty. But he considered this to be shortsighted of MIT: it would in fact help that school by conveying the message that one might join its faculty without necessarily giving up hope of ever making it to Harvard.

Our book did not make quite the splash we hoped for. A Yale humanist reviewed it in *Harvard Magazine*. While he liked it well enough, he took us to task for being insufficiently critical of the spreading blight of grade inflation and for devoting unseemly attention to the grubby topic of how the place was run. A college president laboring under the delusion that I had had a key role in keeping him from the presidency of Brandeis wrote a review for the *New Republic* so vitriolic that his friends prevailed on him not to publish it. (His was an act so at odds with the customary standard of academic morality that it increased my respect for the judgment of those who in fact decided that he wouldn't do as Brandeis's president.)

But the cruelest blow came from a source quite remote from us, or our book. Its publication date was mid-September 2001: not an auspicious time for a work in which Islam or terrorism did not figure prominently. That cut severely into reviews. (In one instance, then-*Boston Globe* reporter Patrick Healy, who covered higher education for the paper, was writing a review when he was told to drop everything and high-tail it to the Middle East.)

People whose opinions mattered to us—among them, economist Paul Samuelson, sociologist Daniel Bell, and historian Bernard Bailyn—thought well enough of the book to keep our *amour propre* from being too badly battered. And the ongoing conspicuousness of Harvard as America's richest, best-known, most-aspired-to university, plus the later un-Harvardian saga of the rise and fall of Lawrence Summers, kept our book relevant. Oxford, its publisher, issued a paperback in 2007 that included an epilogue in which we brought the story down from 2000 to the replacement of Summers by Drew Faust in 2007. Not surprisingly, we found that behind the *sturm und drang* of the Summers storm, early twenty-first century Harvard wasn't changing very rapidly.

The Harvard history put to bed, and (also in 2001) retired from the Brandeis faculty, I turned my attention to that half-sought-after, half-to-be-avoided mode of expression, the Large Historical Synthesis: in this case, of the political history that I had taught and written about for nearly half a century. In my state of soft rebellion against my American history professional identity, I decided to abjure, as much as I could, the rules of the guild. There would be no footnotes; I would try to set the book in the no-man's-land between history and political science; its length, style, and mode of discourse would be aimed primarily at an audience of non-professionals, who might be receptive to history as analysis and explication but had little taste for theoretical apparatus or a heavy-handed academic style.

I started with the idea that this was to be an overview of the whole of American political (and legal and governmental) history, drawing on my career-long reading in the literature of these subjects and on what understanding had come from teaching and writing about them. I put in for a year's fellowship at the

Woodrow Wilson Center in Washington on the assumption that I would draw sustenance from the public policy orientation of the Center and from the city's infinite human and research resources on the subject. That assumption wasn't necessarily wrong; the assumption that my proposal would meet with favor was.

But then a new friend, acquired in the course of American Academy business, rode to my rescue. Nelson Polsby was a legendarily warm and generous professor of political science at Berkeley. He and his hard-driving alter ego Aaron Wildavsky (as Polsby memorably put it, "While I'm sleeping, Wildavsky's publishing") made their Institute of Governmental Studies a lively, welcoming place for students, scholars, and visiting practitioners in politics and government.

Polsby invited me to the Institute and got us an apartment with so spectacular a view of San Francisco, the Bay, and the Golden Gate that it's a wonder we ever took our eyes off it. (Actually, we didn't.) It turned out that Polsby, and Berkeley, were just what my "retirement doctor" (if I'd had one) would have ordered. I was able to bounce my developing ideas about how to write my book off political scientists (Berkeley's historians were not very interested), to its benefit.

As I began increasingly to hang out (intellectually and socially) with political scientists, I became more aware of the subset committed to "rational choice," an approach best described as an attempt to apply the methods and many of the prevailing theories and mindsets of behavioral economics to the study of politicians and political institutions. What made these political scientists and their approach attractive to this historian was their tendency to draw on political history: in particular, the abundant record of congressional roll call votes.

I hasten to add that while their raw material was historical, their purposes were very different from historians'. They were not so much interested in a deeper understanding of the American political past as in drawing on that past for raw material with which to test and refine their theories of political behavior. *Their* past was not so much "a foreign country" in which things are done differently, as novelist L.P. Hartley put it, but (to offer up a more contemporary metaphor) a vast Walmart, in which items of use to the study of political behavior might be picked up.

The rational choice practitioners ("Rats" is the colloquialism favored by their critics) whose work I read, and with whom I interacted, quite rightly found me a babe in the woods when it came to mathematical analysis and economics-based theories. (I suspect that mathematicians and economists regard them with comparable condescension from their more elevated niches in the numerative pecking order.)

But whatever the difference in our objectives, they tended to be more interested in, and sympathetic to, what the thinning band of political historians was up to than were our historian brethren. And the Rats' energy, enthusiasm, and sense of being engaged in a scholarly enterprise that was intellectually challenging and of intrinsic importance was attractive and refreshing, especially when contrasted with the blend of ideology and ennui that I found to be widespread among historians.

But I don't want to romanticize the Rats. Their scholarly output (droppings?) sometimes had a triviality and irrelevance that could seem like a parody of the social-science-as-science model to which they were so devoted. (In a series of conferences on Congress the same papers reappeared, tweaked to take account of the critiques of the previous gathering. After a number of such dry cleanings (three? four? five?) these papers came to be referred to as "tenured.")

Many of the best of the rational choice breed clustered in Stanford's Political Science Department and Graduate School of Business, with a common feeding ground at the Hoover Institution. It is true that the rational choice approach had a relatively conservative subtext in its disinclination to engage in Marxist or post-Marxist (to say nothing of postmodern-deconstructionist) ways of looking at political behavior. Yet what drew them together at the Hoover was not ideology, but (in the spirit of their economics-infused scholarly inquiry) what might be called rent-seeking: reduced teaching, secretarial aid, a laissez-faire research environment, and the other academic goods that an enlightened institution can provide.

In any event, I was asked to come to the Hoover as a visiting scholar for a series of annual stays. This was important to me well beyond the limited time involved. These visits did much to deepen my sense of what the Rats were up to and to integrate that understanding into my American political history rewrite. Political scientists David Brady and Morris Fiorina were especially helpful, buttressing my sense that the best thing an academic retiree who wants to keep sentient can do is to leave his or her longtime disciplinary cocoon and meet new ideas, much as a widow or widower should meet new people.

In 2007 I published *America's Three Regimes*, subtitled with emeritus bravado *A New Political History*. It argued that the four hundred years or so of America's public history might usefully be looked at as falling into three distinctive regimes: deferential-republican, stretching through the colonial and Young Republic years (from the early settlements through the 1820s); party-democratic, through the nineteenth and early twentieth centuries (from the Jackson years of the 1830s to the New Deal of the

1930s); and populist-bureaucratic, from the 1930s to the present, as yet showing no signs of morphing into something else. My not-so-fast view of how American society evolved was summed up in my epigraph, from Finley Peter Dunne's immortal comic character Mr. Dooley: "I see great changes takin' place ivry day, but no change at all ivry fifty years."

I proposed that each of my regimes had a distinctive style or culture, reflected in language, issues, leadership, and the conduct of elections, law, and government. The book was quite favorably received in such toothsome venues as *The New York Times* and *The Economist*.

With the ink barely dry on the paperback edition of *America's Three Regimes* at the beginning of 2009, I embroiled myself in yet another enterprise. As with so many before, it was connected to, but distinct from, what I had been up to previously. It seemed to me that an attempt to track the evolution of what promises to be a major set of public policies, perhaps comparable to the New Deal of the 1930s and the Great Society of the 1960s, was in the cards with the new Obama administration.

I saw in this a golden opportunity for political scientists and historians to apply their theories, *aperçus*, and generalizations, not after the story line was a done deal but as it unfolded. There would also be a fringe benefit: the opportunity to present our findings, in human- (as opposed to scholar-) readable form, to a general audience and to the intermediating pundits, columnists, and the like who sought to explain government to the public.

This met with the approval of the political scientists at Hoover, and five of us created an ambitiously titled Study Group on Critical Junctures in American Government and Politics. The other members are Brady, Fiorina, poli-sci grandee James Q. Wilson, and Harvard congressional guru Kenneth Shepsle. What will come out of it still is very much to be seen. Indeed, my initial contribution to the enterprise, a book entitled *The Unbearable Heaviness of Governing: The Obama Administration in Historical Perspective*, saw the light of publication day shortly before the appearance of this memoir.

So retirement turned out to be not the end of most everything, but the beginning of a new phase of my life, in its way as fresh and invigorating as the move from childhood to young adulthood, and then into a career and the challenge to make something substantive of it. This too was a product of my times as well as of my life. The extraordinary run of ever more wealth, freedom, and opportunity that lay at the core of the American experience from 1945 to (shall we say) 2005—what may be, in history's judgment, the best half century we and our children and our children's children will or could have known—was as responsible for this new life as my luck or talent.

My career (most of it) has satisfied me and, it seems, my family and friends. I have no grandiose illusions as to its impact on the larger world of history, of academia, of America. But no matter. As long as I have (mental and physical) breath, and publishers are complaisant, and there is some interest, however small, Out There in the tale of a quotidian life lived in interesting times, I'm your man. And this book's for you.

INDEX

Other Books by Morton Keller

The Life Insurance Enterprise, 1885–1910

The Art and Politics of Thomas Nast

Affairs of State: Public Life in Late Nineteenth Century America

Regulating a New Economy

Regulating a New Society

Making Harvard Modern
(with Phyllis Keller)

America's Three Regimes

The Unbearable Heaviness of Governing:
The Obama Administration in Historical Perspective